W9-BVI-084

Cofounder of the Shapiro Negotiations Institute, RONALD M. SHAPIRO has negotiated more than $1 billion in contracts. His techniques have helped resolve a national symphony orchestra strike, facilitate solutions to human relations problems, and reconcile disputes in the government and corporate world. His bestselling books include *The Power of Nice*; *Bullies, Tyrants, and Impossible People*; and *Dare to Prepare*.

Praise for *Perfecting Your Pitch*

"*Perfecting Your Pitch* covers a staggering array of life situations, from salary negotiations to personal relationships, in which a wrong word or an inept phrase could mean the difference between success and failure. Sometimes you only get one chance to ask for what you want or express how you feel—and this book is the perfect guide to help you make the most of those opportunities."

—Daniel H. Pink, author of *To Sell Is Human* and *Drive*

"Advice from Ron Shapiro is money in the bank. If you want to learn how to deal with life and business communication challenges, then *Perfecting Your Pitch* is a must-read."

—Ann Curry, NBC News national and international correspondent and anchor at large

"*Perfecting Your Pitch* is filled with powerful insights about effective communication for leaders, parents, friends, spouses, managers, and consumers. Ron Shapiro, a world-renowned negotiation expert, sports agent, and lawyer, shares rich examples and practical wisdom accumulated through decades of experience. The book takes readers behind the scenes of major sports deals, business negotiations, and family challenges, revealing how Shapiro has achieved extraordinary success and helped others follow in his footsteps—all while maintaining impeccable integrity."

—Adam Grant, Wharton professor and bestselling author of *Give and Take*

"Ron's years of experience as a master negotiator, mediator, and coach shine through in this entertaining and useful book. A must-read for anyone facing challenging negotiations and conversations where feelings and identity are in play."

—Robert C. Bordone, Thaddeus R. Beal Clinical Professor of Law and director of the Negotiation and Mediation Clinical Program, Harvard Law School

"Effective, strategic communication is important for success in everything we do. Ron Shapiro is a proven negotiator and renowned communicator, who provides practical advice on how to build individual confidence and deliver hard messages with skill, forcefulness, and empathy. His easily adaptable approach and practical lessons in this great book will help anyone communicate better and more effectively in every walk of life."

—John Harbaugh, head coach of the Super Bowl XLVII champion Baltimore Ravens

"Nothing makes communication more effective than detailed preparation and persuasive delivery. In *Perfecting Your Pitch*, Ron Shapiro provides a commonsense framework to help even the most intuitive communicator improve his or her odds of success."

—Brian C. Rogers, chairman, T. Rowe Price Group

"Ron Shapiro's extremely practical and prescriptive book, *Perfecting Your Pitch*, will empower every reader to have greater control in their lives. In seminary I was taught to script and deliver a sermon: never thought to apply principles of *Perfecting Your Pitch* to every other aspect of my life—husband, father, businessman, and coach. While reading the book I helped my son prepare for a job interview, hired an administrator, and wrote a script for maintaining price integrity of my services while building a relationship with a client. Thank you, Ron—*Perfecting Your Pitch* is a grand slam!"

—Joe Ehrmann, author of *InSideOut Coaching* and president of Coach for America

"As a psychiatrist, I have had my share of difficult communications with patients, their families, colleagues, department chairs, and many others. Using Ron Shapiro's method of the three Ds, I have learned how to prepare a script to help my delivery and also prepare for contingencies."

—J. Raymond DePaulo Jr., M.D., chairman,
Department of Psychiatry and Behavioral Sciences,
Johns Hopkins University School of Medicine

"Three cheers for Shapiro's three Ds. His commentaries on preparation and 'scripting' provide the essential guide to navigating life's delicate situations, ones we all encounter."

—Kurt Schmoke, general counsel, Howard University;
former mayor, Baltimore, Maryland

"This book drips with common sense and rationality. I wish I had this kind of advice when I started my career."

—Warren Green, former president and chief executive
officer, LifeBridge Health

"Sales performance by our team has grown with the implementation of the preparation and principles set out in *Perfecting Your Pitch*. This book is a must for any sales organization."

—John Scanniello, director of Sales Force Effectiveness,
Sherwin-Williams Company

PERFECTING YOUR PITCH

How to Succeed in Business and in Life
by Finding Words That Work

RONALD M. SHAPIRO

with Jeff Barker

A PLUME BOOK

PLUME
Published by the Penguin Group
Penguin Group (USA) LLC
375 Hudson Street,
New York, New York 10014, USA

USA I Canada I UK I Ireland I Australia I New Zealand I India I South Africa I China
penguin.com
A Penguin Random House Company

First published in the United States of America by Hudson Street Press, a member of
Penguin Group (USA) Inc., 2013
First Plume printing 2014

Copyright © 2013 by Ronald M. Shapiro
Penguin supports copyright. Copyright fuels creativity, encourages diverse voices, pro-
motes free speech, and creates a vibrant culture. Thank you for buying an authorized
edition of this book and for complying with copyright laws by not reproducing, scan-
ning, or distributing any part of it in any form without permission. You are supporting
writers and allowing Penguin to continue to publish books for every reader.

P REGISTERED TRADEMARK—MARCA REGISTRADA

THE LIBRARY OF CONGRESS HAS CATALOGED THE HUDSON STREET PRESS EDITION AS
FOLLOWS:
Shapiro, Ronald M.
    Perfecting your pitch : how to succeed in business and in life by finding words that
work / Ronald M. Shapiro, Jeff Barker.
        pages cm
    Includes bibliographical references and index.
    ISBN 978-1-59463-201-3 (hc.)
    ISBN 978-0-14-218122-5 (pbk.)
    1. Business communication.   2. Communication.   3. Negotiation in business.
I. Barker, Jeff.   II. Title.
    HF5718.S457 2013
    650.101'4—dc23
    2013026329

Printed in the United States of America
10 9 8 7 6 5 4 3 2

Original hardcover design by Eve L. Kirch

This publication is designed to provide accurate and authoritative information in regard
to the subject matter covered. It is sold with the understanding that the publisher and
author are not engaged in rendering legal, accounting, or other professional services.
Results may vary on an individual and/or situational basis. If you require legal advice or
other expert assistance, you should seek the services of a competent professional.

While the author has made every effort to provide accurate telephone numbers, Internet addresses, and other contact information at the time of publication, neither the
publisher nor the author assumes any responsibility for errors or for changes that occur
after publication. Further, the publisher does not have any control over and does not
assume any responsibility for author or third-party Web sites or their content.

To those who have entrusted their challenges to me and given me the opportunity to help perfect their pitch

Contents

Introduction
Perfecting Your Pitch—the
Script's the Thing

The West Point cadet and I were in a standoff. I wanted to learn about his studies of negotiations and the simulations he engaged in with stand-ins for village leaders in Afghanistan, while he, a Minneapolis native, couldn't wait to hear about my negotiation of the recent Joe Mauer contract with the Minnesota Twins management. I had come to the military academy eager to speak to the cadets in the negotiation program and to learn about their experiences as cadets, their simulations of war zone interactions with village elders, wailing mothers, and NATO soldiers. But this cadet and many others wanted to hear about negotiating baseball contracts.

Standing in a grand library adorned with pictures and sculptures of renowned generals, I felt the pull of history and realized we were negotiating over who was going to swap his story first.

On the way up to West Point as I looked out the window at the majestic Hudson River during that pleasant train ride upstate from New York City, I was moved as I pondered the experiences and futures of these young people. I knew these men and women were training for potentially life-threatening situations in their negotiating class before moving on to their hardcore military science and math classes, and then subjecting themselves to intense physical training in the afternoons. I realized they would be keen to learn some nitty-gritty sports stories, in part as a relief from all their day-to-day stress.

So I relented and told the questioning cadet—along with a few anecdotes about Joe—about how I had developed a "script" for a critical contract session with Twins management. And then I began to make the connection that inspired this book. Despite the very different situations we were facing, I saw that both the cadet and I would be able to use scripting to ensure that preparation translated into desired results. Because in many of life's battles, large and small, scripting can be an unparalleled tool.

We've all found ourselves in delicate situations—perhaps an important conversation with a spouse, customer, or boss—that seem firmly within our grasp but do not end well or spiral out of control. Days later, we might imagine the salient points we wish we had made if we had planned ahead. But the moment has passed.

I recently was consumed with the scripting for a client who, as controller of a major company, was negotiating with her manager for a long overdue pay raise. Like so many of us, she had no difficulty communicating requests on behalf of others. The trouble was that she struggled when making her own assertive "ask."

In addition, I helped a ninety-two-year-old friend script a forceful counteroffer in a negotiation for the sale of his house. He had arranged to move into a retirement center and was selling his home, but was offended by a lowball offer. It was the only offer he had received for a fine house in a terrible market. However, he didn't know how to effectively state the case for the value of the house.

But when my friend agreed to script his counteroffer, and the controller her pay raise request, using me as their devil's advocate—essentially a coach, ally, and editor—the newfound clarity of their statements and confidence in their delivery dramatically improved their positions.

So, as I stood with the cadet, I smiled and he smiled knowingly, too.

"You know, you may find my negotiations of baseball contracts interesting, but, let me tell you, I find your simulated negotiations fascinating," I said. "They may just save your lives, no?"

It seemed a fitting spot to tell him about scripting. Although it's a tool that could be dismissed as "make-work," scripting is useful in business, in retirement, in our marriages and families, in everyday commerce, and no doubt on the battlefield as well. It links a soldier's high-stakes negotiations with the more mundane battles of regular citizens.

Preparation was the subject of a book I wrote in 2007. In these go-go, high-tech times, publishers had wondered: would anyone want to read about an old-school topic like methodical preparation?

Actually, yes. *Dare to Prepare* was a *New York Times* and *Wall Street Journal* best seller, and I heard gratifying stories from dozens of people who were helped by the book.

But in my travels since the publication of *Dare to Prepare*, the need for this book became clearer. I realized the most critical and overlooked preparation tool was the one that most people resist. Scripting gets short shrift. People prepare well, but perfecting a pitch through scripting requires extra steps and effort at the end of the preparation process that is often neglected. If preparing is running a race, then scripting is crossing the finish line. For me, the mapping out of statements, contingencies, responses, and counters, using a devil's advocate all the while, is the most exciting part of preparation. It can make me downright giddy. And I decided, with this book, to try to spread that enthusiasm.

I came to realize that without scripting, people were left with a gap in their defenses that an opposite party could sense and exploit. My clients and friends identified objectives, researched precedents, and imagined alternatives. But more often than not, if they were unfamiliar with scripting, they fell apart once they arrived at the proverbial table for the discussion. They found themselves "winging it" unnecessarily. On the other hand, when they did script, the added strategic reinforcements changed their outlook. Scripting is the best confidence booster I know.

During the middle of my presentation to the cadets, I caught the eye of my friend the Twins fan. Next to him, a female cadet was already raising her hand.

"How do we make scripting work for us in the context of our negotiations in battle zones?"

Bingo! She'd asked the million-dollar question that her colleague and I had been discussing earlier that day.

The young West Point cadets were likely to go off to war. They were going to be engaging in negotiations with tribal leaders and members of other militaries and irate citizens on foreign streets with stakes that make the commonplace negotiations in life and business seem trivial.

I wanted to show them how scripting techniques that are useful in the most rudimentary situations could be adapted to many of their own life-or-death situations. It's the same process, I explained, whether rehearsing for a budgetary request, selling without sacrificing your price, buying a car, presenting the birds and the bees to our children, settling a debt, offering condolences, firing someone, suggesting a divorce, seeking a job, or marshaling support for an expanded medical research program. These are all make-or-break situations of a sort.

Now before I utter another word, I want to be clear that I am not advocating the end of extemporaneous expression. The vitality of every type of relationship, business or personal, lies in people's ability to express feelings spontaneously from the heart. Ideally we can engage well with others frequently without the scripting process.

Yet the more I spoke to people about scripting, the more I realized how many applications it had. Managers can script before turning down a job applicant or trying to improve their lot with a bullying boss. Salespeople can script to deal with common buyer objections. Consumers can script to prepare themselves for returning a defective product or seeking an airline upgrade. Parents can script before nudging an adult child out of the house or taking the car keys away from an elderly loved one. It's really about preparing for difficult conversations. It's about navigating life.

For the cadets, using a scripting process, when possible, would elevate their success rate, and even their safety. And I admonished them that, as often happens in my examples, all the preparation in the world could fail them if they don't embrace this final critical step before turning thoughts into speech.

That gap—between preparing and presenting, between thinking and speaking—is the Bermuda Triangle of human interaction. And scripting, I believe, is the best tool to bridge it.

My philosophy on scripting is inspired by Abigail Adams. Like many people, I was captivated with the HBO miniseries *John Adams*, based on David McCullough's book. It was entertaining and educational, but, most of all, validating for me both as a professional and as a person. My favorite character, Abigail Adams, became my intellectual fixation, which led me to buy books and conduct research about her. Abigail Adams, as I told those West Point cadets, is my scripting hero. Not because she was a great scripter—that was her heroic husband—but because she was the quintessential devil's advocate. Her husband wrote the scripts for his arguments to convince the Second Continental Congress that the disparate states should mold themselves into the United States of America. Then he tested his arguments on Abigail, who reviewed and revised them. When John Adams ultimately stood up in Congress, the words he delivered to achieve his objectives had been tested, parsed, and improved.

West Point, I knew, instills the convictions of teamwork and dependability. And the cadets in my audience immediately grasped that the young man or woman sitting next to them could be a latter-day Abigail Adams as a devil's advocate. When I speak to audiences, I always ask them, "Who is your Abigail Adams?"

And judging by the murmurs of the cadets, that question really made them think—out loud!

This book, owing much to my exemplars, John and Abigail, and more to my own experiences as a lawyer, sports agent, corporate executive, mediator/negotiator, counselor, and teacher, explains the underlying principles of scripting for successful interactions and compiles a catalog of make-or-break work and life situations and stories that give them context. It then offers model scripts for dealing with each of them. I have selected these scripts based on three criteria: either I have experienced the particular challenge or scenario I am writing about; I have been regularly questioned about a similar situation in my teaching and travels; or I believe this is a situation that readers may face sooner or later.

PART I

✳

The Three Ds: Draft,
Devil's Advocate, Deliver

CHAPTER 1

✳

The Three Ds

Our lives—personal and professional—are full of communications challenges. What's the most effective way to ask for a raise? What's the best way to maintain price integrity for the product or service you are selling? To express condolences to an acquaintance who has suffered a tragic loss? To make an offer on a house for substantially less than the seller has said he is willing to accept? To have a coworker cease sexual harassment? To notify your board that a larger budget is required? To solicit a charitable request from a potential donor? To inform your close friend or relative that you will not be able to help him out with a loan?

How do we deal with communication challenges like these—situations that can be at best sensitive and at worst awkward or intimidating? The words that pop into our heads are often the ones we ultimately speak. Whether at home or in business, there are plenty of situations where it is perfectly appropriate to express feelings spontaneously. But off-the-cuff comments could prove detrimental in other settings. I remember the young executive who described to me his interaction with his boss after receiving a particularly negative evaluation. He described going into the meeting intending to explain to his boss why these issues had arisen and to accept responsibility for the things that he felt related to him.

But, under pressure and unscripted, he fell back on his habits and emotions—a response that many people have experienced in stressful situations. He explained: "The conversation quickly spun out of control as I felt attacked and defensive due to my boss's tone, language, and aggressive manner. In my fearful state, I said some things that betrayed his trust in me and he asked me to leave the building so he could mull over my termination."

Consider also a contract negotiation in which a midlevel executive desires a salary of $100,000. He knows that a basic principle of negotiation suggests that he aim high and ask for at least $130,000. During his conversation with his employer, fear overtakes him and he spontaneously blurts out his request for a salary "in the range of $100,000 to $130,000." He hedges his $130,000 ask with a "range" anchored at $100,000 to soften the blow on his employer's sensitivities. Unfortunately, because we tend to "hear what we listen for," the employer only hears and responds to the lower end of the ask and replies: "I am prepared to pay you $80,000." The spontaneous articulation of a range has disabled the employee's plan to make the employer feel the force of a $130,000 ask.

Is there a better way to thoughtfully craft such important messages—to perfect a pitch? After years of living in the laboratory of successful and unsuccessful communications, I have come to the conclusion there is a process that leads to a higher level of success and satisfaction in the myriad interactions with others that we face in our lives: *scripting*. This tool involves recording our initial ideas and points; followed by critiquing our word choices, clarifying our explanations, and testing our logic; and then choosing the delivery format and practicing to become confident through comfort with the script. It's useful to actively write in bullet or some other short form what you want to convey to the other side. Scripting is a crucial element of the preparation process of negotiation.

In the early days of my career, I understood the negotiation principle that I had to "aim high with reason"—having a good rationale—in making demands. Yet I also feared rejection. Although I would start with a high number in mind, I did not commit to it in a script. So as I spoke, I would retreat to the "range game" and give both the high ask and the number I actually wished to receive. The problem with playing the "range game" is the other side only hears the number closest to his target number and thus starts the negotiation at that number or even below it. In the end, my discomfort with the hard ask and the lack of scripting to overcome it resulted in receiving an amount lower than I had hoped. Learning from this mistake, I trained myself to speak confidently, especially when making a high request, by developing and adhering to an "aim high" script. I wrote down what I wanted to say on a pad of paper, made corrections, studied my notes, and then delivered the ask confidently, with comfort gained by my preparation.

A Big Baseball Contract

Consider negotiating one of the largest contracts in Major League Baseball history. At the time it was signed in 2010, the

Joe Mauer contract was the fourth largest in Major League Baseball history, both in total value and average salary. Despite its magnitude, the process included the same communication issues that arise in so many other situations in our lives—when we say something to people who are not predisposed to hearing what we have to say; when we make a demand well in excess of either their inclination or expectation; when we try to persuade others to buy into an unpopular proposition; when we attempt to wrap an otherwise tense exchange in a cloak of calm demeanor.

All of these challenges and others to which almost anyone can relate surfaced in the contract negotiation I conducted with the Minnesota Twins on behalf of my client, then three-time American League batting champion and 2009 American League Most Valuable Player Joe Mauer. The scripting technique that my partner, Michael Maas, and I employed was an essential piece of attaining Joe's eight-year, $184 million contract and keeping him in Minnesota rather than playing the free agent shell game.

Perhaps the simple, systematic approach for effectively scripting—the three Ds: Draft, Devil's Advocate, and Deliver—is best initially understood when viewed in the context of the Mauer negotiation. In that negotiation, Michael and I faced uncertainties similar to those that others deal with when they must make a request or state a position that they feel the other party may reject. Certainly, we were experienced negotiators, which could have caused us to think we would know what to state, without prior scripting, in meetings or calls with the Twins. At the same time, experience had taught us the value of scripting. After determining that we would have to make an ask at a number ($30 million a year for ten years) substantially higher than where we might ultimately be willing to end up ($22–$24 million a year), I suggested to Michael that he draft a brief script justifying the high target. After Michael completed his draft, I would review and revise it, and we would engage in a back-and-forth devil's advocate exchange. We would weigh possible reactions by the Twins and modify our language where appropriate.

Once we reached a comfort level with the script, it was time for me to prepare for and deliver my ask. Going through the drafting and devil's advocate steps, as well as practicing the script, enabled me to become comfortable with the statement and confidently deliver what could otherwise have been a hesitant presentation.

Founding father John Adams had every reason to be hesitant and sense potential rejection when he sought to move the representatives of thirteen disparate colonies toward a position of embracing the thirteen United States of America. Adams did not merely stand up in front of Congress and deliver his position. Rather, when he rose from his seat in Congress, Adams made his arguments with self-assurance thanks to his delivery preparation, using the drafts he'd developed and the devil's advocacy of his scripts by his wife, Abigail. Following his example, it is important for all of us to deliver our positions with an air of confidence.

But is it worth it to go through the process of the three Ds in everyday life—even when the stakes may seem mundane? While not every transaction involves a multimillion-dollar baseball contract, the outcome of many situations—perhaps an offer on a house or an appeal on a charity's behalf or the resolution of a dispute with an acquaintance—can feel just as important. Losses are personal and hard to take, no matter the arena.

In fact, even my eleven-year-old granddaughter Chloe revealed an awareness of this during a complicated situation with a friend. Chloe had been close with this friend, whom I'll call Lisa, since they were four. Starting in kindergarten, the two had the same group of five friends and these close friendships continued into their preteen years.

But the summer before entering the fifth grade, a change occurred. A few of the girls in Chloe's tight-knit group created a system of sleepovers every weekend that summer without thinking about how their exclusive sleepovers affected others— particularly Chloe. Meanwhile, Chloe was busy that summer visiting family and other friends. As a result, the fifth grade began in a somewhat awkward way for Chloe, as she was feeling slightly insecure about her friendships with her favorite group of girls.

Needless to say, there were strains and, for the first time ever, real trouble in the friendships. Lisa started to neglect her friendship with Chloe and to focus instead on fitting in with her other classmates, sometimes at Chloe's expense. Eventually a combination of gossip and separation appeared to take the friendship to its breaking point, making the need to talk more important than ever.

Chloe and her mother, my daughter Laura, decided that since emotions were running high, the best thing to do was to write down a list of the points she wanted to make to her friend. Along the way, Laura, as Chloe's devil's advocate, suggested as her only piece of advice that Chloe start each sentence with "I feel" because no one can argue with the way you feel.

Once Chloe's emotions had cooled she gained confidence by practicing what she was going to say. Chloe made a note card with a list of issues she felt that she and Lisa needed to work through and the points she wished to raise. On the other side of the note card, she wrote encouraging words to make herself feel stronger. On the front of the card, Chloe had scripted the issues, followed by various prompts. She wanted Lisa to remember how close they were and how she had always kept Lisa's secrets. Her words of encouragement on the back of the card read, in all caps, STAY POSITIVE, I CAN DO THIS, BREATHE, KILL THEM WITH KIND-NESS, BE-YOU-TIFUL YOU, and finally, BE LIKE POPS. The final encourager—a reference to me—obviously touched me deeply.

She practiced for her conversation with Lisa by reading her points to her mother a few times. When she left the room—and during the drive to Lisa's house—Chloe continued to read the "strength" words to herself. Chloe felt that her encouraging word list calmed her and was as important as the actual message. Equipped with this note card and a good-luck charm, a locket with a picture of her with her sisters, Chloe was ready to deliver the script to her best friend.

Although there were lots of tears, Chloe remained calm and confident throughout the conversation. She expressed her feelings and apologized for the things that Lisa said she had done that hurt her. Chloe repeated several times: "I love you, Lisa, and would never want to intentionally hurt you. I am so sorry you felt that way." Chloe made all of her points to Lisa. Although it was awkward for a couple of days following this emotional exchange, the two rekindled their friendship, and while Chloe never fully reentered the original group of five, she and Lisa have remained close friends.

Everyone wants to become a better communicator, but the question is, are they willing, like Chloe, to do what they have to do to get there—to practice the three Ds?

There is an adage that everyone knows what they are supposed to do in pursuit of better health—do not smoke, eat plenty of fresh fruits and vegetables, get enough sleep. The trick is actually following these steps. Likewise, it is the act of gathering all of your thoughts and emotions regarding the situation on paper, then selecting the strongest points and weaving them together in order to create a cohesive dialogue, that, once practiced, allows you to communicate your feelings and opinions effectively.

Keep in Mind:

- Scripting in crucial conversations usually leads to more successful communications.
- Draft, Devil's Advocate, and Deliver are the three steps of the scripting process.
- Scripting can be used in challenging situations in both your business and your personal life.
- With extemporaneous expression, it is easy to be misunderstood or be too emotional—scripting helps control that.
- To be confident in delivering your message, put it in writing and have it cross-examined by another. This will raise the level of its clarity and its impact.

CHAPTER 2

✳

Draft

Drafting what you wish to say is an important step in creating your strongest possible argument. It is the process of getting your raw ideas and all of your feelings out in the open without such potential negative effects as being misunderstood or letting your emotions get the better of you. In emotional situations, drafting is therapeutic because it gives you an outlet to say what you need while increasing the likelihood of achieving the desired outcome.

Imagine yourself facing the challenge that Michael and I dealt with in the Mauer situation. Our research revealed that there might be a market available to Joe that could have led to a contract of ten years at $30 million a year, perhaps more. Of course, this assumed he stayed healthy and performed at his MVP level for another full season before entering the free agent sweepstakes. If his performance declined in the following season, he could suffer a decline in his market value. That is similar to someone thinking about selling her house at the height of real estate values in 2007—then waiting another year for an even higher market value only to discover that the bubble had burst. We also had some negotiation principles to follow, such as trying to get the first offer from the existing team. The Twins did offer Joe an extension of five years at $18 million a year. Using the aim high with reason principle, we had wanted to make an offer that we sensed might well be beyond anything the Twins, even with their new stadium, would absorb within their payroll framework. We (including Joe) all had strong opinions about what he was worth.

We also knew that Joe wanted to stay in Minnesota for the long haul. He grew up in Minnesota and lived there, as did most of his family. The Twins drafted him first overall and he loved the fans and the community that supported the team, but he was also curious to discover how other teams perceived his value and what it would be like to test the market for the first and maybe only time in his career.

After probing and ascertaining that the club understood Joe might command $30 million a year in the open market—and weighing the risks of waiting for the market and consulting with Joe—we decided upon an ask of a nine-year extension at $27 million a year, for a total of $243 million. While that may not have been our final figure, every principle of good negotiating suggested it was appropriate. It was akin to the practice of listing a house for an asking price above what might ultimately be an acceptable selling price. If the price is too unreasonable, there is a risk of scaring away potential buyers. For this reason, it is essential to have a well-researched basis justifying the first offer. In Joe's case, he was a rare commodity—a catcher with the best offensive and defensive skills in the game, a team leader, and the holder of several major-league hitting records at a young age. As a result he was the most unique potential free agent of the crop, with his primary market risk being that of an injury.

While Michael and I knew our initial counterproposal for $27 million a year was well beyond where the Twins had suggested they might go, the key was to remind them that the team would have to raise their ceiling in order to keep Minnesota fully competitive. At the same time, we decided we did not need to further convince the Twins that Joe on the free agent market could command a historic contract in the $300 million range. We also wanted to include in the conversation a player option, which would allow Joe to terminate the contract if the team did not stay competitive. Winning—and playing in the World Series—was important to Joe. This provision was likely to stir negative reactions in the club.

After researching all considerations, Michael drafted a short and simple script that we would ultimately shape for use in a meeting with the Twins' senior vice president and general manager, Bill Smith:

> Bill, your proposal of a 5-year extension at $18 million a year is unacceptable. Joe has a chance to get twice that in the free agent market, and is unwilling to give so much up to do a deal now. While he might consider a hometown discount, it would be more in the range of several million dollars, and the contract would also require an option out for Joe and a strong package of performance incentives as well as trade protection. Joe's unique achievements certainly warrant that.

After the draft was completed, but well before the delivery, it needed to be vetted in the devil's advocate step. The initial draft laid the foundation and forced us to sort through the various ways—long, short, story laden, etc.—to proceed. For example, should the script be brief and to the point, illustrated by stories, or lengthy and full of detail? The initial draft was fairly blunt, lacking in specifics, and perhaps too brief. Devil's advocacy would correct that.

So the first step—draft—does not require much more than translating your views into a rough position statement to sketch out what you want to express to the other party without worrying much about whether it is the best way to say it.

Our Mauer strategy has a variety of everyday applications. Take someone suffering a problem common to today's workplace—a woman whose work schedule has been cut from forty to thirty-two hours a week along with a reduction in compensation. She was told how important she was to the organization, but that her reduction was for economic reasons. Let's call her Lindsay. Her job was to sell and manage events at her company's facility.

In the summer of 2011, Lindsay contacted me with her problem. She was frustrated and angry enough to demand that she be restored to full pay, yet insecure enough to feel that she should not rock the boat. Lindsay had also recently been informed that her son Tyler, who was beginning his freshman year at the University of Maryland in the fall, did not receive the financial aid package they had hoped for. The amount of money needed to support her son's education was now going to become a debt that would only increase annually. Tyler's current part-time job as a waiter would not cover the remaining tuition, and Lindsay did not want Tyler to further divert his attention from his studies. Lindsay was concerned that her son would not have the college experience she had hoped for while following his dream of becoming an architect.

I suggested that she script out what she would like to say to have her hours and pay restored. I told Lindsay not to worry about what she said in the draft script, but rather to simply express her feelings and desires.

Lindsay was full of excitement when she brought her draft to me. She felt she had artfully presented all of her concerns on how she was being treated by her boss and she hoped for my quick approval of her "brilliant" statement. In actuality, she, not unlike others I have dealt with, provided me with a wordy draft shaped more by emotion than reason.

Here is her initial draft (I have condensed it for our purposes and, as with many of the scripts in the book, made minor corrections and omitted the company's name):

> It is my hope that my dedication and commitment to the company is abundantly clear to management. Since the cuts last year in March, I have given everything I had to make sure events and their execution would be beyond successful—I don't think anyone would question that success.
>
> Over the past year and a half I have put my own personal and financial well-being at risk by going far, far beyond the call of duty in my commitment to the company. By the sheer nature of my responsibilities at the company it means that my work hours continually change and that I must work many weekends and evenings . . . I work seven days a week in odd jobs to manage the cuts made to my hours and salary. By observations of family and friends I am told that I work entirely too much and that it is unhealthy to not be fairly compensated for all the time I give . . . When I am not in the office I am still always taking calls, being responsive to needs, and keeping balls moving through my personal cell phone and my home office. It is part of my core being to give all I have to give without thinking of much in return. As I grow professionally and

personally I am recognizing that it is only right to be fairly compensated . . .

It is unreasonable to expect of me to work as a salesperson and events manager to my fullest capacity in balance on part-time hours on a 20% pay cut. It was negligent to a degree to expect me to do this . . . and not recognize a burnout point. In order to perform my role with the company well I must be incredibly responsive and available far beyond the normal workday or workweek. I have done this through sheer faith, the ability to work very hard, and courage of conviction to the company without industry-standard commission compensation of 2%–5% on sales at the very least or even a full-time base salary . . .

. . . I am so far beyond spread thin it is beginning to rattle at my emotional levels of feeling resentment and anger toward the company—feelings I never want to have but they are growing. I don't know how I can properly carry out sales, staffing and administrative functions while continuing to have a real personal life and making financial ends meet at the end of the month . . .

In addition, I have my son's future to worry about. At my present rate of pay, I greatly fear we will not be able to afford college and have him live up to his full potential. The amount of support the school has provided him falls short of what we need.

Restoring full-time hours with appropriate salary and compensation will allow me to tap into and grow these areas of income and contribute to the financial well-being of the company even greater than I currently do while being fairly compensated and allow me to meet my financial responsibilities.

Lindsay had stated her case—in words that were sometimes contradictory and emotional. It was clear she believed she was being taken advantage of and was frustrated with her employer.

While her underlying anger would be camouflaged in her ultimate delivery script, it served a useful purpose at this stage of releasing stored resentment while beginning to frame her case. It is important to acknowledge such anger—at least to yourself— but not necessarily to act it out. Sometimes the act of writing an angry message or e-mail can be emotionally cleansing. But do not hit the Send button. Anger comes from the heart, but the negotiation strategy—and remember it is just that, a strategy— needs to come from the head.

One man who understood this was Abraham Lincoln. America's sixteenth president engaged in a similar therapeutic process during the Civil War. When he was disappointed with one of his generals after an unsuccessful battle or other failed military action, he at times would write an angry rebuke to the general. Yet instead of having the letter delivered, he would deposit it in a desk drawer. The act of stating his frustration with the man's actions gave Lincoln the emotional outlet he needed without deflating his military leadership at a time when he had no alternate in place. So these "Lincoln letters," as they have been called, became a useful place for venting anger without prematurely taking action.

Unlike President Lincoln, however, Lindsay needed more than a therapeutic release. She needed action almost immediately and hoped that the script she had drafted was the perfect way to ensure she received what she needed. Imagine, then, how Lindsay felt when she saw me pick up my red pen and begin to line through and make notes on what was a powerful presentation. As difficult as it was for Lindsay to watch, I was carrying out my role as a devil's advocate. Clearly, her initial draft was not intended to be the perfect delivery document. The second phase of the three Ds, Devil's Advocacy, would improve the draft just as it would for Michael and me in connection with Joe Mauer's negotiation preparation.

Keep in Mind:

- Drafting is a vehicle for stating any and all thoughts for your message without regard to whether you ultimately use all of them.
- Drafting can be a good safety valve for bottled-up emotions.
- Remember the Lincoln letters.
- Be ready for constructive input.

CHAPTER 3

✳

Devil's Advocate

The devil's advocacy step in the scripting process is based on the premise that all of us can improve how we do things—in this case, communicate—by having others review and provide input for our work. This is a variation on the old saying that two heads are better than one. Sometimes we are just too close to a subject to sense how our words affect others. While drafting allows us to gather all of our thoughts pertaining to the situation, we still need a devil's advocate to supply frequent reality checks and help us adjust the message. Just as a good miner sifts dust and other unwanted material from the gold, the devil's advocate works to separate the ambiguous asks, muddled emotions, and weak rationales from effective points and powerful statements.

When I draft a script, I seek out my Abigail Adams, whether it is my wife, Cathi, for personal matters; my law partners Paul Sandler or Larry Gibson for legal challenges; my partner in our negotiation firm, Todd Lenhart, for business deals; or my sports agency partner, Michael Maas, for the Joe Mauer contract and an array of other transactions. In those rare times when I don't have access to a devil's advocate, I read the script out loud to myself—acting as my own devil's advocate.

Chapter 2 reveals how writing out a draft of the script may get to the substance of what you want to say. Yet that first draft may frequently lack the right tone, sound too emotional or defensive, or be phrased in a manner that prevents it from achieving maximum effectiveness. Remember the title character played by Tom Cruise in the 1996 movie *Jerry Maguire*? In a binge of late-night emotion, he crafts and distributes a "mission statement," only to think better of it in the morning. His sentiment may have been pure, but he regrets not having reviewed the document—or having someone else look at it—in the sober light of day.

How often does a salesperson harbor the same regret, introducing a proposal, without first seeking reaction from his team members, and watching it fall flat? Perhaps with a devil's advocate, the idea might have been improved in a way that would have landed rather than lost an account.

In the Mauer negotiations, I served as Michael's devil's advocate after he gave me his draft of the counter to the Twins. I might add that in any given situation Michael may act as devil's advocate for some of my drafts and I some of his; the roles can alternate. In the case of Mauer, I gave Michael back his initial script, marked up as follows:

Bill, we have taken your proposal of a 5-year extension at $18 million a year to Joe. ~~is unacceptable.~~ If he signs an extension, he is making substantial concessions in that he is forgoing the free agency process, though testing the market could possibly lead to a bidding war that would result in one of the largest contracts in baseball. After speaking with Joe, we believe that a contract extension for 9 years at $27 million a year is an offer he would be willing to accept. ~~Joe has a chance to get twice that in the free agent market, and is unwilling to give so much up to do a deal now.~~ We believe Joe is worth more and if he goes to free agency, he could very well receive a contract much larger than we are proposing. ~~While he might consider.~~ He is willing to make this offer at a hometown discount. Since we are doing this for the club, ~~it would be more in the range of several million dollars, and~~ the contract would also require Joe would like trade protection as well as an option ~~out for Joe and a strong package of performance incentives~~ to terminate this extension if the club stops being committed to staying at a competitive level or if the market for players changes significantly and makes this extension inappropriate for a player of Joe's caliber. ~~unique achievements certainly warrant that.~~

In revising his draft, I focused on changing the phrasing of sentences to make our claims more factual rather than simply personal opinions. In addition, I sought to explain our actions—and why they supported our request—instead of simply stating what we wanted in a contract. This approach made our demands definitive and our reasons understandable.

Devil's advocacy can be an ongoing process; more than one redraft may be developed during this second stage. Michael and I talked more about this script for Bill and made further changes. Here are Michael's edits to the script I returned to him:

Bill, we have taken your proposal of a 5-year extension at $18 million a year to Joe. If he signs an extension, he is making substantial concessions in that he is forgoing the free agency process, though testing the market could possibly lead to a bidding war [Do we mention NY and Boston specifically?] that would result in one of the largest contracts in baseball [Do we name numbers?]. After speaking with Joe, ~~we believe that~~ a contract extension for 9 years at $27 million a year is an offer he would be willing to accept. We believe Joe's **value is greater,** ~~is worth more~~ and if he goes to free agency, he could very well receive a contract much larger than we are proposing. He is willing to make this offer at a hometown discount. Since we are doing this for the club, Joe would like trade protection as well as an option to terminate this extension if the club stops being committed to staying at a competitive level or if the market for players changes significantly and makes this extension inappropriate for a player of Joe's caliber.

In this round, rather than revising, Michael raised questions about possible additions to the script. And our discussions of these questions led to contingency provisions that would later appear in the final script.

As a result of the devil's advocacy process, this script was far more specific than the original, the language was better suited for negotiations, and we had touched on more points for discussion. Through this stage, Michael and I reached a point at which we were ready to start preparing for delivering the message to Bill Smith and the Twins' front-office team.

In Lindsay's case, there was more work to be done in modifying the draft because Lindsay, like most, was not an experienced negotiator. She had a practiced devil's advocate in me. Generally one can find an effective person to fill the role. The ideal candidate may be a friend, relative, or colleague, as long as it's someone who will not hesitate to offer critical input. Even better is someone who has experienced a similar challenge. It is important that the devil's advocate make suggestions and offer criticisms in a manner that does not trigger a defensive reaction. Lindsay needed to make her point more succinctly and with persuasive language rather than aggressive statements or emotional appeals. Once she got over the shock of red ink, Lindsay carefully read and considered my marked-up version, which included my comments (in brackets) as well as suggested deletions (struck out) and additions (in bold):

I want to spend a little time talking about my job and compensation at the company. Since the cuts last year in March, I have given everything I ~~had~~ **have** to make sure **rentals, our large annual event, other development** activities and their execution would be beyond successful—I don't think anyone would question that success.

The problem is that over the past year and a half I have put my own personal and financial well-being at risk by going far, far beyond the call of duty in my commitment to the company. ~~By the sheer nature of my responsibilities at the company it means that~~ **My job requires that** my work hours continually change and that I must work many weekends and evenings. **And because of my reduced compensation, I have had to work different odd jobs to bridge the salary/needs gap.** ~~I work seven days a week in odd jobs to manage the cuts made to my hours and salary~~ By observations of family and friends ~~I am told that~~ I work entirely too much and ~~that~~ it is unhealthy to not be ~~fairly~~ **adequately** compensated for ~~all the time I give~~ **my job here.** [Are you working hours at the company in excess of those you are compensated for???] **You should also know that** when I am not in the office, I am still always taking calls, being responsive to **event** needs, and keeping balls moving through my personal cell phone and my home office. ~~It is part of my core being to give all I have to give without thinking of much in return. As I grow professionally and personally I am recognizing that it is only right to be fairly compensated . . .~~

~~It is unreasonable to expect of me to~~ **I cannot be expected to** work as a salesperson and events manager ~~to my fullest capacity in balance on part-time hours on a 20% pay cut.~~ **with high impact on a part-time schedule and a 20% pay cut.** [Is the 20% based on gross or rate??] ~~It was negligent to a degree to expect me to do this . . . and not recognize a burnout point. In order to perform my role with the company well I must be incredibly responsive and available beyond the normal workday or workweek.~~

[What follows is confusing. Is this your call to action or further elaboration? Should it be edited down to a sentence and included as an example of the grievance above??? Needs clarification . . . rewrite in light of question . . .] I have done this through sheer faith, the ability to work very hard, and courage of conviction to the company without industry-standard commission compensation of 2%–5% on sales at the very least or even a full-time base salary . . .

[Similar comment to immediately preceding paragraph: Can we condense the two into a simple call to action that maps out your ask—perhaps a bit higher than you are willing to accept—and also restates the reason relating to the reality of your job and your personal needs??] **In the past I have never been an hour counter—I do whatever it takes to get the job done. I am now sacrificing my own integrity of thinking and I start counting hours because I am feeling taken advantage of and not being fairly recognized for the hard work, talent, and dedication I bring to the company.** I am so far beyond spread thin it is beginning to rattle at my emotional levels of feeling resentment and anger toward the company—feelings I never want to have but they are growing. I don't know how I can properly carry out sales, staffing, and administrative functions while continuing to have a real personal life and making financial ends meet at the end of the month. **This is not even taking into account new initiatives I am involved in . . .**

In addition, I have my son's future to worry about. At my present rate of pay, I greatly fear we will not be able to afford college and have him live up to his full potential. The amount of support the school has provided him falls short of what we need.

Restoring full-time hours with appropriate salary and commission will allow me to tap into and grow these areas of income and contribute to the financial well-being of the company even greater than I currently do while being fairly compensated and allow me to meet my financial responsibilities.

Lindsay had been heartfelt in her draft, but when I put it to the test of devil's advocacy, it was in need of a number of things. She exhibited a fear that created a sense of defensiveness. At the same time, she seemed in attack mode. Either might affect her ability to deliver her message when the time came. I advised her to soften and shorten her arguments either through rephrasing or deleting. As I read through her original script, I was uncertain of her intent in some areas. Instead of putting words in her mouth, I asked that she explain exactly what she wanted to convey to her employer. I asked her to clarify her logic in her own voice.

Lindsay, like most, had been entangled in her emotions when she wrote her first draft. While she appreciated my input, she did not relinquish her emotions easily. We spent some time not only validating some of her feelings, but also redirecting her thought process. As I sat across from her, I saw her eyes glisten and heard her voice quiver now and then. I continued to reassure her that we were engaged in a process to help her achieve her employment goals and to support her son's education.

With time and encouragement, she seemed to relax and became more clear-eyed as she gradually understood what scripting was really about. For Lindsay to achieve her goals, it was not necessary to attempt to shame the boss for his treatment of her. Instead, our objective was to explain logically and professionally to her employer her request for full-hour and compensation reinstatement.

Going through this scripting process greatly lessens the amount of miscommunication that will arise during an actual meeting. Since the intended audience may have a very different vantage point, this stage allows someone else (the devil's advocate) to consider that perspective in shaping the ultimate demand. The script above was only the first in a rewriting process that would eventually conclude with Lindsay's finished product (set out in the next chapter), which I supported. Once Lindsay had drafted a final script, she was ready to practice her delivery to her employer, just as Michael and I were for our meeting with Bill Smith.

Keep in Mind:

- Having a devil's advocate helps you take your initial thoughts and modify them to most effectively communicate to the other party.
- Devil's advocacy can be an ongoing process; more than one redraft may be developed before the final script.

- Your devil's advocate should ask you questions about your draft, seek clarifications, and then offer suggestions for deletions and additions.
- If possible, keep your devil's advocate involved until both of you are satisfied with the script.

CHAPTER 4

✳

Deliver

The third D, Deliver, helps you avoid uncomfortably delivering the hard "ask" by familiarizing yourself with the final script. In order to deliver convincingly after you have written and edited what you wish to say, you must become comfortable with your script so that you may deliver smoothly. By rehearsing aloud, preparing for interruptions, and establishing confidence with what you want to say and how you are going to say it, you effectively implement the last of the three Ds. It is also helpful to find someone, perhaps your devil's advocate, to act as a delivery coach who will listen and prepare you for interruptions. If you make your case without confidence, your intended audience will sense weakness and therefore not feel obliged to agree with your statements or correctly understand your feelings if you are discussing personal matters.

The actual conversation may occur in different contexts. In some cases, such as over the phone, you can keep the script in front of you during the delivery. In a face-to-face meeting, you may have to deliver from memory. Television reporters often hold their notebooks during live interviews below the shot and out of the view of the people at home. These notebooks serve a scripting function. On the pages are lists of questions, and perhaps follow-up questions or talking points. There is symbolic value to carrying the notes: the interviewer literally does not want to come to work empty-handed. By practicing for the interview, the news reporters are prepared to address the main points of their story clearly. Similarly, the rest of us may want to come equipped with a list of bullet points or even a full-blown script as a reference. But the most important thing is to have internalized the material by that point.

There are situations, however, in which you should not bring your script or notes along because they could signal a lack of confidence. These cases require additional practice delivering the script. This step can be viewed like a dress rehearsal for a Broadway show, in which the assigning of roles and construction of the sets have already been completed and now it is time to perfect the pace of the actors' lines and their stage presence. This step is invisible to the audience, just as the efforts that go into practicing the script delivery will be unseen by the receiver. The end result on opening night, or when the meeting occurs, is a strong performance.

While this metaphor of a Broadway dress rehearsal describes a thoroughly practiced delivery, it may be helpful to consider elements of improvisational theater. Just as actors in improv do not know exactly how their fellow actors will respond to their dialogue, you cannot know exactly how your audience will react to specific parts of your statement.

Similar to actors, lawyers during a proceeding can be caught off guard. I have admired some lawyers' aplomb during U.S.

Supreme Court oral arguments. A first-time observer to the Court's viewing gallery may assume that arguing a client's case is as simple as giving a speech. It is not. The lawyers are frequently interrupted by justices' questions and comments, getting only a few words into a thought. They must thoughtfully and politely address the justices' concerns without losing sight of the big picture, and continuously return to making their case. Their preparation for the hearing involves research and careful scripting. It is likely that multiple scripts will be developed in order to ensure that all the potential stages of the hearing are addressed.

Just as it is common for court cases to last weeks, the same is true for landmark sports contract negotiations. We knew that the day we opened discussions with the Minnesota Twins would not be the same day we closed the deal. It took a series of phone calls, followed by meetings in Minnesota and during spring training in Florida, before a contract was signed.

Although I have a lot of experience with delivering scripted messages, I still use Michael to assist me with preparing for the actual delivery. For those who are less experienced, it would be beneficial to find an acquaintance who challenges you as you deliver your script. It is possible that your devil's advocate will also be your delivery coach and prepare you for the actual conversation. The objective is not only to enter the conversation confidently but—when asked a question—to counter confidently as well.

This is the script Michael and I had perfected for the first formal meeting of the negotiation. The script includes reasonably high goals and some "wish list" terms that might have stirred hesitance in their communication if we did not practice our delivery and receive the comfort and confidence that comes with it.

Bill, we have taken your proposal of a 5-year extension at $18 million a year to Joe.

If he signs an extension, he is making substantial concessions in that he is forgoing the free agency process, though testing the market could possibly lead to a bidding war [hold on mentioning NY and Boston specifically, unless subsequent discussion requires] that would result in one of the largest contracts in baseball [if required, name numbers: as much as $30 million a year for 10 years]. After speaking with Joe, a contract extension for 9 years at $27 million a year is an offer ~~he would be~~ **we are** willing to accept. We believe Joe's value is greater, and if he goes to free agency, he could very well receive a contract much larger than we are proposing.

He is willing to make this offer at a hometown discount. Since we are ~~doing this~~ **making this accommodation** for the club, Joe would like trade protection as well as an option to terminate this extension if the club stops being committed to staying at a competitive level or if the market for players changes significantly and makes this extension inappropriate for a player of Joe's caliber.

The scripting process led to the development of a script that not only supported our point, but also was brief enough for me to embrace and express with confidence. And, although Bill never told me, he might have even appreciated a bit of brevity.

As expected, there were multiple stops and starts in the contract talks after the first meeting. The Twins initially said they would move off their initial proposal, but not to where we wanted.

The media's focus on the proceedings and outcome of the deal complicated negotiations. During the talks, Michael and I took steps to avoid being spotted by reporters. The media would try to glean meaning from basic information such as our whereabouts. When we went to spring training to visit with our clients, including Joe, the media spun stories focusing on the negotiation and created stories about "talks heating up." As we stepped off an airplane in Fort Myers, Florida, a reporter saw us. Before we knew it, there was a headline in the *St. Paul Pioneer Press* three weeks before Joe signed: "Mauer's reps visit Twins camp." As the meetings continued, we practiced the principle of not negotiating in the press. It was hard enough to make a deal with the other side; adding a third party that would inject their thoughts would unnecessarily complicate this process.

This first script began the negotiations at a dollar figure that, while rational, was uncomfortable to ask for because of its historically large size. It was essential, however, that we begin the negotiation at such a number, because it laid the foundation for what was, after sequential meetings, ultimately a successful negotiation. Over the span of working toward an agreement, we created multiple scripts for multiple meetings, engaged in back-and-forth conversations with the Twins, and addressed every detail of the contract. In the end, we were able to sign Joe to what was the fourth-largest contract in Major League Baseball history at the time. It was all thanks to the hard work by the Twins, a strong commitment by Joe, and some pretty effective scripting. On the day the deal was announced, with his parents and two brothers sitting nearby in the Lee County (Florida) Sports Complex, Joe signed an eight-year contract extension at $23 million per year using the same pen with which he had signed his rookie contract in 2001. "Wow," he exclaimed after signing the deal to remain playing for his hometown team through the 2018 season.

Lindsay's situation, in contrast to Joe's, was not a game of high-stakes sports negotiation. Rather, it was everyday life, much like what most of us experience from time to time. Her scripting process involved fewer steps and did not quite garner the same amount of media attention. But it involved a similar process. Lindsay—the event manager frustrated because her hours and pay had been cut, and worried about her son's future— never had to refer to the script during the discussion with her boss because of how thoroughly she rehearsed. The tool gave her direction and confidence in her delivery.

This is Lindsay's final script. When she delivered her message it was not verbatim. Instead, the script served to organize her thoughts and offer a foundation for practicing delivery so that she could respectfully and effectively communicate her message.

I want to spend a little time talking about my job and compensation at the company. Since the cuts last year in March I have given everything I have to make sure our large annual event and **other** development events and their execution would be **activities are** beyond successful—I don't think anyone would question that success.

The problem is that over the past year and a half I have put my own personal and financial well-being at risk by going far, far beyond the call of duty in my commitment to the company.

My job requires that my work hours continually change and that I must work many weekends and events. And Because of my reduced compensation, I have had to work different **multiple** odd jobs to bridge the salary/needs gap. **I work seven days a week.** By Observations of family and friends **are that** I work entirely too much and that it is unhealthy to not be adequately compensated for my job here. You should also know that when I am not in the office, I am still always taking calls, being responsive to event needs, and keeping balls moving through my personal cell phone and my home office—**all without compensation . . .**

I cannot be expected to ~~work~~ **perform with high impact** as a salesperson and events manager ~~with high impact~~ **on a part-time schedule and a 20% pay cut.**

I have done this ~~through sheer faith, the ability to work very hard, and courage of conviction to the company without industry-standard commission compensation of 2%–5% on sales~~ **without even asking the industry-standard commission compensation of 5% on rental** sales at the very least or even a full-time base salary . . .

~~In the past I have never been an hour counter—I do whatever it takes to get the job done. I am now sacrificing my own integrity of thinking and I start counting hours because I am feeling taken advantage of and not being fairly recognized for the hard work, talent, and dedication I bring to the company. I am so far beyond spread thin it is beginning to rattle at my emotional levels of feeling resentment and anger toward the company—feelings I never want to have but they are growing. I don't know how I can properly carry out sales, staffing, and administrative functions while continuing to have a real personal life and making financial ends meet at the end of the month. This is not even taking into account new initiatives I am involved in . . .~~

In addition, I have my son's future to worry about. At my present rate of pay, I greatly fear we will not be able to afford college and have him live up to his full potential. The amount of support the school has provided him falls short of what we need.

[Wait for response. If appropriate: "Do you understand my dilemma?"]

So what does it all come down to? Restoring full-time hours with appropriate salary and commission will allow me to tap into and grow these areas of income and contribute to the financial well-being of the company ~~even greater than I currently do while being fairly compensated and allow me to meet my financial responsibilities~~ **and it will allow me to meet my financial responsibilities without working multiple jobs.**

Like a presidential candidate participating in mock debates, Lindsay and I simulated the encounter she would have with her boss by creating a similar environment in my office. I remember that when Lindsay initially read her script, she was tentative and nervous. "Let me hear it again with less hesitation," I instructed. After she had read it a few more times I said, "Let me hear it again, but don't look at it." As she grew comfortable with the text, I began to challenge her by interrupting her with statements like, "I know where you stand on this." She was momentarily flustered, but after more practice she became capable of working through distractions and returning to her points.

Once she had mastered her presentation in spite of my interruptions, I started to throw questions and unforeseen responses into the mix. As she learned to deal with them, we also wrote down a list of "possible answers" that she could study to be prepared for "unforeseen" contingencies. (See "Preparing for Varying Scenarios—Contingency Planning" in chapter 5.)

While there would have been no harm in Lindsay having her script in front of her if the discussion occurred over the phone, I wanted her to internalize the document. Although scripts can be memorized, I did not want the presentation to come off as robotic or for her to seem thrown off if she was interrupted.

My goal as Lindsay's delivery coach was for her to practice keeping her mind engaged as the meeting unfolded. You can never truly know how the other side will respond no matter how many hours you devote to preparing. Even the best campaign advisers cannot foresee every scenario that might unfold during a candidates' debate. Nevertheless, Lindsay was sufficiently equipped and thus felt reasonably sure that she was ready for almost any eventuality when she met with her boss. And if she felt stumped by a question or comment, I advised her that she could always retreat with "Can I get back to you on that?"

Unlike lawyers in a Supreme Court oral argument, Lindsay was rarely interrupted by her boss during her delivery. She was able to say what she wanted and articulate to her boss her frustrations. A restoration of her hours and $12,000 of her salary was made along with better delegation of responsibility. Although this was a smaller increase than she had hoped for, her boss— moved by the challenges regarding paying for her son's tuition— introduced her to a local service club representative. A month later, the club awarded her son scholarship funds to supplement tuition. Lindsay was satisfied, because she believed a positive change had been made: her boss had demonstrated support, and she now had help and more money of her own to contribute to her son's college tuition.

In both cases, we started with a goal. Chief among Joe's was to continue his career in his hometown of Minnesota at a salary close to the market rate. Lindsay's focused on being more equitably compensated for the time and effort she devoted to the company. The two substantially achieved their goals by applying the three Ds (Draft, Devil's Advocate, and Deliver). Both scripts were working documents. Language had been honed and streamlined in each. While a contract negotiation, asking for a raise, and other situations that involve a challenging request can be acrimonious, we wanted to avoid any lingering ill will. When Lindsay approached her boss and when Joe's representatives entered their negotiations, they had to be prepared for contingencies. Their scripts needed to be flexible game plans to account for unexpected twists and they had to be presented confidently. The trick is to know the material well enough so that you are comfortable with it, but not to have it so prepared that it loses a feel of spontaneity and sounds rehearsed.

Part II, which follows, presents various examples in which utilizing the three Ds allows you to comfortably and effectively present your thoughts, whether it be to sell your product, make your case, offer advice, or express a feeling.

Keep in Mind:

- By practicing script delivery, you lay the foundation for effective communication and build a comfort level with your message.
- Being comfortable and speaking with confidence makes your position less vulnerable to the other side pushing back. Your audience is less likely to give you what you want (or close to it) if they sense hesitancy in how you state your case.
- Before going into a meeting take a deep breath and remind yourself that you are prepared and ready to deliver the message.
- The actual conversation may occur face-to-face, over the phone, or via e-mail.
- For situations that don't play out in person, it is okay to have your script in front of you. Speak naturally when delivering it. In some circumstances, do not display your script in face-to-face meetings because it may diminish your perceived confidence. If necessary, you can refer to some bullet points on a pad or card.
- It is helpful to find a delivery coach who challenges you as you practice.

- Be prepared for the coach to cut you off as you practice delivering your script to prepare you for possible interruptions and questions.
- Remember it is not only what you say, but also how confidently you say it.

PART II

✳

Model Scripts

Selling Seinfeld

As I was putting the finishing touches on this book, I received a call from my good friend Steve Mosko, the president of Sony Pictures Television. Steve wanted to give me his reaction to a video I had sent him that was a mini pilot for a reality show that another friend of mine had developed.

Steve asked me how I was doing, and I told him I was in the homestretch on a book to be submitted to my publisher the following week. When he asked what the book was about, I explained the theme of *Perfecting Your Pitch*. He reacted immediately by reminiscing about programs I had taught to his organization and how, as a result, scripting had become a part of his business arsenal.

He then asked me if I had seen the preceding week's *New York Times* story about an Internet show, *Comedians in Cars Getting Coffee*, a production that Jerry Seinfeld is producing with Sony Pictures Television for its multiplatform network, Crackle.

Steve gave me the background, telling me how, when Sony

initially made the presentation to Seinfeld, it was competing with powerful Internet firms that were also pitching Seinfeld for the business.

What Steve did to prepare for his presentation is revealing. He wrote out a script.

Steve explained: "I was ready for them. You should've seen the notes and ideas that I scratched out on my pad before my meeting with Jerry. I thought through all aspects of what would be important to him and what was important to us, and I plotted them out like a script. And when I went in to make my presentation, I felt fully prepared and able to address the issues that were important to Jerry. Ever since you and I discussed the principles of preparation and scripting in your programs, I have embraced them in my work."

The script became the blueprint to deliver Steve's message that Sony Pictures Television was the right partner for Seinfeld on this project. Steve had contemplated in advance what the concerns of his potential partner might be. He wanted to convey to Seinfeld that he had an appreciation for the differences between *Comedians in Cars* episodes—which run eleven to seventeen minutes—and traditional television.

In his scripted pitch, he described his company's capability and willingness to use appropriately novel approaches to execute an innovative project like this. Finally, he underscored the importance of his company's resources and flexibility.

In the television business, Steve is probably more familiar with traditional scripts of the sort read by actors. This script was intended to be more flexible—a well-crafted guide. In creating such a script, Steve made the same calculation that many of us make when we must prepare high-stakes presentations at work or home. He simply decided that there was too much on the line to risk a misstep.

I couldn't help but consider Steve's scripting the best sort of endorsement of the process. Steve understood that even the most capable and influential executives aren't served by merely improvising. Better, he thought, not only to have devised a clear negotiation strategy but also to have already articulated and parsed the words he intended to use. Like a quarterback walking through the game plan, he had a clear vision before the discussions began.

Hopefully the model scripts and stories that follow will help you to attain your goals in many of your challenges, in business and life.

About the Scripts

The following chapters provide forty script examples to serve as models for a variety of situations involving communication challenges, both business and personal. While the model scripts should not be used verbatim, they can serve as starting points for tailoring a script to meet particular challenges.

The model scripts, in most cases, are the product of the three-Ds process, developed through the Draft, Devil's Advocate, and Deliver steps to meet the issues described in each chapter. To avoid redundancy, the three-Ds process is not repeated in these model script chapters. Consult part I if you need a refresher on how to implement the three Ds.

While reading the upcoming chapters will enhance your skills in dealing with communication matters, you may also refer to them to guide you through specific situations. In the final analysis, your message and delivery will be more effective when you combine using the process of the three Ds with taking specific cues from the examples that follow.

Scripting is a tool to use in the business world to get what you want while maintaining positive relationships. It can also be a useful aid to communicate effectively in the context of your most emotional or complicated personal challenges. Making a budget request, pitching yourself for a job, terminating a lease, intervening with an addict, breaking up with your boyfriend, denying a relative a loan—the following pages can offer guidance for creating the best possible script and ultimately a statement of your position or feelings.

Scripting can seem like a time-consuming process, but these model script chapters should help expedite it. They will, to the extent they are applicable, put you at a greater advantage for your upcoming conversation and provide you with suggestions for what should and should not be said. In the short amount of time it takes to read a chapter and write down a few notes, you may exponentially increase your confidence and ultimately the effectiveness of what you say. Keep in mind the scripts are models for your messages. Use them as suggestions or catalysts for what you might say in order to help build the most effective platform for your message. Several scenarios in the following chapters may require medical, psychological, or legal counsel. This book does not purport to offer expertise in those areas, but rather focuses on the kinds of communications that may apply after a decision to take action has been made with the assistance of a professional adviser.

In most cases scripts will be delivered orally, in person, or by phone. In some situations, however, the context may suggest another medium, such as e-mail. If the other party has e-mailed, an e-mail response may be appropriate. Other types of communication, such as offering condolences to the bereaved or inquiring about one's status after a job interview, may dictate sending a letter or e-mail.

We've divided the scripting chapters in part II into sections. The sections are arranged to start with the business and professional arena and move on to media, family, friends, and consumer concerns.

CHAPTER 5

⁎

Sales Challenges

Selling but Holding Your Price

A customer or client may sing praises for your product and his firm's relationship with you. At the same time he may insist that you reduce the pricing of your product or services to maintain that relationship.

Some sales teams then spend time thinking about where to make cuts and how to reduce prices to satisfy the customer's demand. The best course, however, would focus on how to maintain the relationship and at the same time not compromise pricing integrity. This may require some good old-fashioned research and analysis of the client's needs and marketplace alternatives. If such research reveals that you are the right fit and best alternative for the client, then scripting may be a useful tool in protecting your pricing and renewing the client's business.

The script is used to craft the message to the client on the benefits of the product or service you offer and why pricing should remain at its current levels or, perhaps even better, be increased. In some sense this requires ignoring the client's statements about the need for price reduction—a negotiations approach in which you seek a result that the customer has suggested he will not accept. It can be unsettling for a salesperson or account executive to come back to a client with a proposal that ignores the client's demand for a price reduction.

The scripting process helps overcome such trepidations and builds a comfort level in the position to be expressed. The more confidently the seller states her side's thoughts or position, the more likely it is that the buyer will recognize that getting a reduction is not achievable. The expression of the seller's position should not be an "in your face" statement, but rather an attempt to help the client achieve his objectives without losing sight of the importance of the seller maintaining her pricing and margins.

※

A professional sports team that is a client of my Negotiations Institute had a long-standing relationship with a corporate sponsor—a real estate brokerage firm. The sponsor enjoyed the affiliation with the sports team, and also got substantial exposure in the marketplace with prospective commercial and residential real estate clients. On a number of occasions during the past five years, the sponsor had spoken approvingly of the market position it had been able to achieve through the affiliation with the team.

Nevertheless, with six months remaining on the sponsorship agreement, the real estate company's president informed the team's account representatives that it would have to receive more inventory and a 25 percent reduction in pricing in order to continue the relationship. The inventory in the sponsorship package included signage in the stadium, advertising in the team's programs, promotion on the electronic scoreboards, and a suite that the real estate firm could use to entertain clients. The pricing of the package was $500,000 per year. In addition to the requested price reduction, the real estate brokerage suggested that it would also need in-game radio ads as well as more prominent signage included in the deal if it was to go forward with the team.

Although there were other real estate firms in the marketplace that the sales team might call upon as alternatives to this client, the team really desired to hold on to the relationship because of the brokerage's prominence and long-term connection with the team. Some of the sales team felt that they should provide the client with the additional inventory and try to minimize the reduction to something in the range of 10 to 15 percent.

We advised the team's corporate sponsorship group that their offer to the real estate firm ought to take some of the inventory off the table while emphasizing to the client the real benefits of the relationship, such as the exclusivity in the client's business area. We also suggested to the sales team that they present a price *increase* in order to be consistent with other contracts being executed with sponsors—perhaps in the range of 15 percent.

After some resistance for fear of losing the account, the corporate sponsorship group agreed to pursue our recommendation. The sales executives also agreed that in this case a written proposal would express the team's position with clarity and a certain level of unambiguous definitiveness. We then asked them to script out how they would make the initial presentation to the client, and after several rounds of devil's advocacy the following e-mail on team letterhead was developed:

Dear [Client],

The [sports team's] brand within the region is strong and is growing. Last year special events and concerts were added and over 80,000 flocked to [our athletic facility] to enjoy them. Customized activations and marketing programs were created. Attendance is up 36% vs. 2010, TV ratings are up 108% vs. 2010, radio is up 59% vs. 2010, page views on [our website] are up 119%, and Facebook Friends are up 118%.

Simultaneously, the [sports team's] brand association and return on investment for partners is strong and growing. Numerous awards have been won by our marketing and promotions staff for marketing initiatives and in-game entertainment execution. Vendors have experienced double-digit sales growth. Within the past season we have added over a dozen new corporate partners and have had record in-season partnership sales. To deliver the most effective and valuable experiences for our fans and partners, we will continue to create and enhance opportunities. Some recent examples are programs for kids and social media initiatives.

Due to the factors above, the [sports team] has increased team expectations in regard to the value of team assets and exclusivity in partnerships. Due to the competitive nature of the marketplace, we have identified the real estate brokerage category as one where we must grow revenue with current partners and/or secure additional partners.

You have stated your need to reduce the financial investment in our partnership. At the same time, however, you should know that while we can adjust your investment terms, we are unable to maintain assets or exclusivity on a flat or reduced investment.

Please see the attached spreadsheet that has two options for your review. Option A, with a price increase of 15%, maintains almost all assets from the previous agreement, and also includes several additional assets which you requested. Option B, which uses your current pricing level, includes reduced assets and the elimination of exclusivity for your suggested investment level.

We hope you find one of these options acceptable and look forward to the continuation of our mutually beneficial relationship.

Best regards,

[Team Executive]

After several more rounds of discussion and scripted face-to-face presentations (which denied the real estate company's continuous requests for inventory increases and price reductions), a deal was made. Much to our client's surprise, not only was the team able to actually hold the line on inventory, but it also achieved a 10 percent increase in the pricing of the sponsorship package for the next five years.

In fact, the team executives who led the negotiations later commented on the impact the scripting had on their success and said, "We reached a deal that was considerably above our highest goal and strengthened the relationship. The preparation, the scripting, and the counsel were outstanding." They also said, "Not only did the scripting process produce an immediate return on investment; it also implemented a systematic approach for us to negotiate future deals more effectively."

Keep in Mind:

- Rather than just think about where to make cuts and how to reduce prices to satisfy the customer's demand, focus on how to maintain the relationship while not breaking pricing integrity.

- Have a thorough knowledge of the marketplace so you can compare your situation, as much as possible, with similar situations.
- The more confidently you state your thoughts or position, the more likely it is that the buyer will accept that getting a reduction is not achievable.
- The scripting process reduces the seller's insecurity stemming from ignoring the customer's demand and builds a comfort level in the message.
- The expression of the seller's position should not be an "in your face" statement, but rather an attempt to help the client achieve its objectives without losing sight of the importance of the seller maintaining its pricing and margins.

Creating an Objection Planner for Sales Teams

Most of the scripts in this book are designed to meet the challenges of a specific situation. This chapter is a little different. Sometimes it is useful to develop scripts in advance to respond to recurring situations we face.

For example, I have worked with organizations in a variety of industries in which salespeople must deal—on a recurring basis—with objections raised by potential customers. A home builder may have to deal with questions about room size, proximity to schools, curb appeal, or even doorsill heights. An insurance broker may be queried about the appropriateness of a policy for someone of the prospect's age, premium levels, or other insurance products compared to whole life insurance. And car salesmen may have to be ready for pricing objections based upon Blue Book or other dealer quotes, questions about the value of extended warranties, or delivery times and service issues.

The salespeople must develop blueprints to confidently rebut competitor claims, unsubstantiated rumors, or consumers' misunderstandings about the products or services they are selling. The best preparation for this challenge often involves developing a script with peers in the same situation. Proposed answers can be drafted and shared with team members. After some group "devil's advocating," an "objection planner" can be developed that members of the sales team can turn to as a script for guidance. Caution, however, should be exercised not to use the ready-made "planner" responses as an excuse to go on automatic pilot. Never stop listening to the customer. What the other side says may contain shades of difference from the objection you prepared for.

✳

Before the affinity credit card pioneer MBNA merged with Bank of America, I and others from our Negotiations Institute trained MBNA workers, including members of the business development team, in negotiation and influencing skills. I worked particularly with managers negotiating deals in which MBNA partnered with potential and renewing affinity credit card partners, including alumni associations, university athletic departments, high-visibility retailers, and trade associations. In its negotiations, MBNA needed to sell these and other groups on why it was the best bank to acquire or renew the organization's endorsement. The endorsements involved, among other things, putting the organization's name and logo on the credit card and being able to market the organization's member or customer list. MBNA would, in turn, offer the group compensation based on account activity and marketing programs to the group's members or customers to activate accounts. Guarantees or advances against future earnings were also sometimes part of the package.

Because of the intense competition among bank card organizations—and due to MBNA's market dominance—the competition floated rumors and leveled attacks against MBNA and its credit card product. After discussing the situation in our training programs, we noted that the attacks and rumors fell into a pattern. For example, it became common for an association to suggest that it was being offered a less favorable deal than other associations—that its prestige was being disrespected. Or that MBNA rotated account executives too often, was so big that the potential group would feel lost, or indulged its executives extravagantly so as to reduce the pot of potential compensation for the group.

Once we established what we were up against, we set out to develop the right words to counter what we were hearing. The objection planner for the four issues noted above looked something like the following.

Issue: Is my compensation structure in line with schools that are considered to be my peers?

Possible response: [Ask: Which schools do you consider to be your peers? Why do you consider them to be your peers? What are the factors you use to compare yourself?]

We work hard to keep compensation for like programs consistent; however, just as I'm sure you wouldn't want us discussing your compensation with your peers, we prefer not to discuss theirs with you. In fact, we're all contractually obligated not to discuss contract specifics with others. I will say that we take a lot of factors into consideration when developing a financial offer, including the types and cost of the products that we will be offering to your members, the size of the list, access to marketing channels and venues, . . . the strength of the affinity, and the historical performance of the portfolio. We're happy to discuss how we can increase your revenue stream using these factors.

Issue: I have had x account executives over the past x years. It's like a revolving door at MBNA, and that hurts our ability to develop a strong relationship.

Possible response: [If you're likely to hear this objection, know what the previous account executives are doing today and be prepared to discuss. You may also want to be prepared to discuss continuity as it relates to your sector or regional director since they tend to move less often than AEs. You should also develop some examples of new ideas that have come from either a new AE for this program or another one in the sector. If you personally started on the phones at MBNA, tell that story. Know your success stories.]

We're just as interested in building a strong relationship as you are, and we believe that we have one. Can you offer me some examples of when a change hurt the program?

Our approach is by design. We promote from within, identifying outstanding people who learn the business from our customer satisfaction, customer assistance, and credit areas and having them work directly with endorsing organizations. They bring different experiences to the table and understand the organization. The new AE brings new insights, fresh ideas, and experiences from other areas of the bank (in many cases, the new AE can apply lessons learned in a different sector to your program), which will help you build your asset, i.e., get more accounts, increase loans, increase royalties, and perhaps even add members.

Our approach stresses continuity while fostering creativity and innovation . . . Many of our senior managers were account executives and marketing managers at one time, and they bring that experience and understanding of group needs to their jobs.

Our commitment to you is that there will always be a good person managing your program.

Issue: You treat us like a small fish in a big pond. You have too many groups, and we feel as if we're not important to you.

Possible response: [Ask where the group heard this. If it was a competitor bank, ask whether the group would like to see a list of other large groups that chose to move their programs to MBNA from that competitor bank over the past year. It's also very important that you know what MBNA has given the group over the years as a way of focusing on how it dealt with the group on an individual basis. Ask if we failed to meet its needs. If we have, ask for examples.]

MBNA's core focus is credit cards, and has been since 1982 when we opened with 15 endorsing groups in an abandoned A&P supermarket. Today, we are much larger—we . . . have endorsements from more than 5,000 groups—that's 5,000 votes of confidence from endorsing organizations about MBNA's ability to meet their needs and the needs of their members. We are experts in the affinity business. We had the same concerns you expressed as we began to grow. That's why we created smaller businesses by grouping similar endorsing groups such as colleges and universities and professionals. This enables us to focus our marketing efforts and apply lessons learned with one organization to others within these "sectors." Then, as we continued to grow, we built upon the sector approach by opening regional offices to get closer to our customers . . .

Our credit process is another example of our focus on the customer . . . Using credit analysts to make decisions, rather than letting the computer do that job as other large issuers do, enables us to focus on each customer, one at a time.

Issue: MBNA spends a lot of money on luxuries. I heard a lot about your airplanes, yachts, or cars.

Possible response: That's not the first time I've heard that, but let's talk about perception versus reality. We have one large boat we use for entertainment purposes—ours is, after all, a relationship business. We have a couple of corporate jets—just like many Fortune 500 companies (and fewer than most)—so that our executives can get quickly to our regional and international offices and to our customers. We have some antique automobiles that we use in our marketing because prospective customers are drawn to them when we market at events, particularly ones in the motor sports sector . . .

These scripted answers to common objections helped build the business developers' confidence in responding to customer concerns. The objection planning process was frequently an effective tool for the developer to solidly make the bank's case to a new endorser or one contemplating renewal. Even when not successful, team members benefited from their collaboration with their peers in developing the scripted answers in the planner. They felt increased confidence in making points to hesitant renewal prospects and potential new customers.

Keep in Mind:

- Common customer concerns or objections may best be dealt with by objection planner scripts.
- Collaborative peer efforts in building and working out responses through devil's advocacy can lead to effective messaging.
- The objection planner "possible responses" are a foundation for more confident answers to customer concerns.
- Embrace the planner points, but not at the expense of listening and properly matching the response to the concern.

Preparing for Varying
Scenarios—Contingency Planning

How often have you gone into a meeting with a plan of action, only to find that the challenge posed by the other party is not what you expected?

You're like a quarterback approaching the line of scrimmage and finding the defense in a different scheme than was anticipated. At that moment, you only hope you've adequately planned for contingencies and can seamlessly shift to a suitable play. You sure don't want to have to wing it.

It's the same in sales. You may plan for a particular client response and get another. This section shares some concepts with "Creating an Objection Planner for Sales Teams," above. But the situations are different. In this case, you are engaged in a specific sales transaction. In the other, you are developing answers to a generic set of sales objections raised by potential buyers. The key in this circumstance is to contemplate alternative reactions to your proposal by the client and then "Draft, Devil's Advocate, and Deliver" a response to each possibility.

If you're not prepared with contingencies, you may appear to be surprised and hesitant in responding. Creating backup plans allows you to confidently address the client's position, improving the likelihood of achieving your objective.

In 2011, a broadcast radio client of mine sold a $100,000 sponsorship package to a major medical system for the launch of its new state-of-the-art cancer facility. The inventory in the package included blanketing morning and afternoon drive times with commercials and allowing the medical system significant participation in the station's health fair. That would give the cancer center the opportunity to interact with the public at a well-attended live event.

The chief marketing officer who made the buy for the health system expressed satisfaction with the program and planned to make a similar buy for another of the medical system's centers the next year.

Halfway through the campaign, however, the CMO left and was replaced by another executive with whom the broadcaster's sales team had little familiarity. When the sales group leader made contact with the new CMO, she was told that her group could make a presentation. But she was also informed that the CMO had other priorities and might only be able to give the team an initial visit and follow-up meeting before he made his decision "on where to go with the station."

The sales team recognized they may have limited opportunity to make their case and that preparing a single proposal could miss the mark. So they prepared a "contingent series of scripts" to prepare for their meeting. They also were well schooled in probing and were ready to ask questions about the CMO's objectives if given the opportunity. In the final analysis, they wanted to be ready not only to move forward with the relationship, but to deal with whatever direction the CMO pointed. They scripted the following four scenarios for this initial meeting.

Scenario 1—CMO informs us that the medical system wants to keep all inventories the same for 2012

"We are happy to hear that everyone wants the partnership to continue for 2012 but thought that the medical system would consider adding to the inventory due to the success of our partnership. What are your objectives for the 2012 campaign? We will analyze the 2011 package and see if everything can remain as is for 2012. Are there any proposed changes to the time slots and programming plan we followed previously?"

Scenario 2—CMO informs us that budgets have been trimmed and the medical system will need to rework the inventory, but its preference is to reduce the package but stay linked to the morning and some afternoon drive time

[In this case, probing at this initial meeting may better serve our purposes.]

For example, we could ask, "What is the reason for the budget reduction? What did the medical system have in mind when it suggested the need to rework inventory?"

Then: "Obviously this is disappointing and we will need to reevaluate the relationship should the medical system lower its investment. Are the elements of our partnership covered by a specific radio sponsorship budget or are they part of the overall media budget?"

Then: "Let us get back to you."

Scenario 3—CMO informs us that the medical system would like to do more in 2012 to brand more of its services and become more active with the partnership

"This is good news. We also want to see this relationship continue to grow. What are the elements of programming and additional demographics you are looking to add? Have you set a budget at this point? In any event, let us do some analysis based on financial information you give us and let's see what kind of package we can craft to serve your objectives in 2012."

*Scenario 4—CMO informs us that due to managerial
changes and budget shifts the medical system is not going
to be able to renew its partnership with the network*

"How was this decision made and what other budgets have been
affected? What led to these changes and what is happening with
other sponsorship/marketing initiatives? Hypothetically speaking, if you had it in the budget, would you support a spending
amount with us similar to that of 2011? Why not let us put something in front of you should you change your mind?"

Other points to be addressed that are not necessarily scenario specific:

- If asked about a multiyear agreement or the category outlook past 2012—we will ask, "How many years?" And then
  we will state that all options are being explored and we
  want to talk to all interested parties at a future date about
  the opportunities that could exist.
- We might ask, "Is the medical system considering any new
  media partnerships in the market in view of the leadership
  changes?"

After acting out the various scenarios among themselves, the
sales team members felt ready for almost anything. What they
encountered was completely unexpected. Instead of meeting
with the CMO as anticipated, the team ended up in a session
with the medical system's advertising agency account manager,
who excused the CMO's absence due to other commitments.

This was a scenario the sales team had not planned for. But the
team was not thrown off balance. The account manager opened by
saying that the medical system was inclined to continue with a

radio campaign at the station—but because of reduced budgets it would be a more limited campaign. This triggered the probing questions of scenario 2.

The team had been initially taken aback by the CMO's absence. But they recovered quickly and were able to get information from the account representative that allowed them to put together a new package with reduced afternoon inventory, but no price reduction. The team suggested that if the medical system did not buy the time slots, there were other health care organizations that would. As of this writing, it appears the medical system will also be renewing for 2013. The CMO, however, has remained as elusive as ever to the broadcast sales team.

Keep in Mind:

- Contemplate alternative responses and brainstorm contingent responses to each.
- Draft proposed responses that best address each of the contingencies. Where relevant, prepare probing questions.
- Consider omnibus questions that may be asked regardless of the scenario that unfolds.
- Deliver a confident response whatever route the client or customer may take.

Fund-raising to Receive a Large Donation

Few people are comfortable asking others for money. Even fundraising experience and a good cause do not necessarily diminish discomfort. Board members, school or college alumni, friends and family of a person afflicted with a disease, and an array of others may feel a strong attachment to a charity connected with their cause. And yet while understanding the importance of the cause may inspire them to action, making the request of a potential donor, whether in person or by telephone, remains difficult. The scripting process may empower the fund-raiser to meet the challenge and hopefully lead to the potential donor contributing to the cause.

The best fund-raisers don't just make the ask—they begin with some probing questions directed at learning about the potential donor and his or her giving interests. Asking questions may also contribute to building a relationship between the donor and the fund-raiser. The answers to the queries may ultimately shape the request. Whether they do or not, the solicitation must be delivered with deference, but firmly. A request for funds should be pegged at an amount above the actual need. Doing so, though uncomfortable, is facilitated by scripting the ask. Even the most giving donors are inclined to make a gift that falls below the request.

Information relating to the potential donor's giving history and interests, visual aids, and the cause's appeal will all play a role, but the message scripted and delivered is the ultimate solicitation impact point.

Having the right script will help turn a reluctant or meek fund-raiser into an effective spokesperson for the cause.

✳

A few years ago I was approached by an attorney friend, Sean, who sat on the board of a leading teaching hospital. He explained that he was charged with seeking significant support from a financial institution that had recently established a presence in the community. The goal was to persuade the bank to make a $1 million "naming" contribution for a stem cell transplant center at the hospital, meant to aid in the battle against a variety of cancers, autoimmune disorders, and hematologic diseases.

Extensive research revealed that the financial institution supported hospital causes in other cities and that its chair had real interest in cutting-edge cancer treatment. Despite the encouraging information, Sean was uneasy making a solicitation of that magnitude. Imagine, then, the level of his discomfort when I suggested that to gain the $1 million objective, he should ask for $1.25 million because the foundation's board had a history of trimming requests directed to it.

Sean and I honed a script that supported his confident solicitation. We met with the executive director of the bank's foundation as well as its regional president. During our meeting we spent some time talking about the bank's growth since moving into our area and asked questions to learn about recent foundation activities. At that point, Sean smiled and began to deliver our ask.

> We appreciate your giving us the time to tell you about our hospital's proposed stem cell transplant center. We also want you to know how happy we are that your bank has joined our community.
>
> In order to give you a real sense of the impact the center will have in the battle against certain cancers and other diseases, I want to show you a brief video about the project that demonstrates the necessity of the center. [Play the video.] Do you have any questions?
>
> [May have to modify the following if assumptions change based on answers to the opening probing questions.] Now, let me tell you what we propose. We would like to call the center the [Bank's Name] Stem Cell Transplant Center. It's

going to take $2 million to get the center up and running. We are asking the bank, as the naming rights partner, to underwrite $1.25 million of the cost. Here is a detailed budget for the project. [Hand over a sheet of the detailed budget.] Do you have any questions?

We know your institution makes a big difference in the communities it serves. The [Bank's Name] Stem Cell Transplant Center will lift the level of health and well-being of its constituents in our community. It's projected that the center will be able to significantly aid those suffering from a variety of diseases, especially cancer. The bank can join the hospital in creating a healing place for many. We hope you agree.

Thanks for your consideration and feel free to reach out to me if you have any questions.

[May insert prior to departure:] By the way, do you have a timetable for making a decision on the project?

Before leaving, Sean and I were told that we would have an answer within ten days. In half that time, Sean received a hand-delivered letter informing him that the bank's foundation was happy to support the creation of the stem cell transplant center with a contribution of $800,000 to be paid within two months' time. The letter also stated that the bank wanted to participate in all decisions relating to publicity with respect to the contribution and the dedication of the center. That was welcomed by Sean and the entire university medical center fund-raising team. Afterward, Sean showed me that he had carefully folded a copy of the script for the ask and placed it in his wallet as a model for future asks.

Keep in Mind:

- Research your potential donor ahead of time and if possible begin the interview with some further questions.
- State a connection point that addresses the donor's interest, if any, in the cause.
- Clearly express the impact contributions have on the cause.
- Support, when appropriate, with visual aids and/or printed information.
- Aim high with reason.
- Practice the script to build confidence and reduce apprehension about asking for money.

CHAPTER 6

✴

Managerial Challenges

Making a Budget Request

Budgetary requests address a variety of needs. A teacher may need supplies for a project he wishes to launch with his students; a designer must know what resources she will have available for a job; or a department manager seeks budget support for new initiatives he is planning.

Regardless of a person's profession, whether he is an academic, artist, or attorney, there will come a time when the challenge of making a budget request is essential to accomplishing an objective.

Budget requests require effectively communicating needs and their rationales. This presentation may be performed alone or, if the setting allows, with a group of peers to reinforce it. The approach to seeking specified amounts will often be similar to asking for a raise. You aim above the goal (with reason) with the expectation that the funds or resources budgeted will be less than those asked for.

In crafting such a script, it is important to research budgets previously addressed by the decision makers—past budget expenditures approved, as well as denials. Further information about how these individuals manage the process will be helpful. This information can help to fine-tune the approach to making the ask. The devil's advocate step is particularly important to effective budgeting in order to thoroughly prepare for questions the decision makers might ask or concerns they might raise about the request.

The budget requester should be prepared to ask plenty of probing questions, too. If you're told that your required funds will be denied, consider asking the following questions: "Are there any other sources of funds or resources that could supplement the budget?" or "Hypothetically speaking, if you could find the funds, would you support the program?" By asking questions and seeking further explanation, you may learn something that increases the chances for reopening a request and arriving at an acceptable compromise. Finally, delivering a message confidently, which comes from practicing the script, could give your request a forcefulness it might not otherwise have.

※

Recently Barbara, the chair of neurology at a major teaching hospital, felt her department needed renewed financial support from the university to maintain its high level of esteem and the significant impact it had in research and patient care. She identified two major needs of the department—acquiring fifteen thousand square feet of additional wet lab space and successfully recruiting a researcher and a clinical leader for her team. This would increase her departmental expenditures by as much as $450,000 per year, plus require "dowry" funds of $3 million to lure the two new world-class team members.

Having participated in one of my negotiation seminars, Barbara came to me for assistance in crafting an effective budget request. After some discussion and a review of past actions the university's CFO had taken, Barbara and I concluded that her ask would have to be at least 10 percent higher than she required. The CFO had a tradition of cutting 10 percent from budget requests. We crafted the proposal so that it was fully justified even with the additional 10 percent based on precedents from other departments. Barbara knew from the budget process from when she was originally recruited as chair that it was important not only to make a firm request slightly in excess of her ultimate goal, but also to gain a *firm commitment*. She had learned a valuable lesson from an earlier experience when she was told she would receive ten thousand square feet of additional wet lab space for her research team; in actuality, she received an allocation of only five thousand square feet. Therefore, a written confirmation of the commitment became a part of the request.

It became clear that not only was the request essential to the proper functioning of the department, but if Barbara did not receive the required financial support, she would feel invalidated and possibly consider moving on. Although Barbara was at first skeptical of the scripting process, we followed the three Ds in textbook fashion. When it came time to help Barbara practice delivering her final script, we did so in a meeting with several other delivery coaches—leaders in her department—so that the script would be tested by people knowledgeable in the ways of the medical school, as well as by my experience negotiating budget requests. Despite its medical context, the final script was not much different from scripts prepared in other contexts.

I know that you go through this process with many other department heads and it's probably second nature to you. I can tell you that it is never comfortable for me to ask for money when I'm asking for myself. But when I'm asking for the department, I do so for the good of the entire institution. We have been rated among the best departments in the country and to keep that rating and our high impact level, we need to do certain things that require financial and space support from the medical school. [Before I go further, do you have any questions about the department's operations or its accomplishments at this point?]

There are two components to my ask. The first is funds and the second is wet lab space, both of which are equally important. We need to immediately recruit a researcher and a clinical leader for the department, which will require additional support of $495,000 per year over the next three years—anything less will deny us the ability to maintain the high level of cutting-edge research and patient care for which we have become known. Here is an operations plan that demonstrates that level of need and use of funds. [Hand out the plan.] We will also need reendowment funds, which I will discuss in a minute.

We need an additional 17,000 square feet of wet lab space to continue our present research projects and initiate two other vital programs—they are an essential piece of our overall research plan. The space has to be as close to contiguous to the department's existing research space as possible. When we last asked for research space we received from your predecessor a significant commitment that was never carried out. Hence, I would also ask that the space be committed to the department in a written memorandum that states delivery dates as well as its location.

The operations plan contains a complete description of our wet space needs and plans, the research position and the clinical leader position, which I have described to you, as well as a onetime dowry commitment of $3.3 million to lure the best and brightest to the new positions. It also gives you a quick overview of the significant accomplishments of the neurology department in the last four years. [Do you have any questions?]

I hope I have made clear the department's needs and that the department's request will be fully satisfied.

When Barbara finished making the presentation, the CFO did not indicate his support—or lack of it—for the request. He asked a few questions and informed her that he appreciated her effort and needed to spend some time with the dean to consider the proposal. Barbara left the meeting somewhat discouraged by his lack of commitment. But that cloud evaporated a week later when she received a call informing her that she would be allotted the necessary financial support and $2.5 million in dowry funds for the new faculty she sought and three-quarters (12,750 square feet) of the wet lab space she desired. In addition, she was told she would receive a confirmation letter within the week.

Although Barbara was originally reluctant to engage in the process of scripting—possibly feeling it below the job description and experience level of an esteemed medical department chair—she moved from hesitance to happiness and ultimately gave full endorsement to the process after her objectives were substantially granted. Barbara was finally able to plan her recruiting process and map out the move of members from her research team into the new space. She now considered the scripting process an instrument in her department chair's medical bag.

Keep in Mind:

- Script in detail the needs you want to address as well as the funds and resources you seek.
- Aim high—with reason.

- Research the decision maker's precedents and comparable situations prior to making your budget request.
- Use your peers as devil's advocates or delivery coaches. Ask them to join you in the meeting if their presence is strategically meaningful and acceptable to the decision maker.
- Maintain a calm demeanor even if the decision maker does not appear supportive.
- Do not take a denial personally. There is not an endless supply of funds.

Denying a Budget Request

As corporate budget makers know all too well, it's not just accumulating money that can be challenging—it's parceling it out. Anybody who manages an organization appreciates it is a limited resource that must be reasonably rationed in the business and personal worlds. Every organization has to set a budget for each of its operations and divisions to ensure that tasks are adequately financed and ultimately performed. With any budget request, the issue may simply be who gets what. But how that decision is communicated often presents a challenge.

Whether denying all or part of a request, the message has to be delivered clearly and sensitively so the turndown is understood and the requester is left only minimally frustrated. Motivating people to perform at the highest level is a key component of leadership. The leader doesn't want to deflate his or her team with a harsh denial (except perhaps in the case of frivolous requests, which are not the subject of this chapter).

The scripting process will facilitate crafting a clear and respectful communication.

The key to a smooth budget denial is a well-expressed rationale. A subordinate who is given a rational basis for being turned down is likely to feel better about his organization and his manager than one who believes his carefully constructed request has been summarily dismissed. Spending some time crafting the denial—and then trying it out on another manager—will build a better case that can serve as both an explanation and a guide for future conduct.

It can be useful to convey a sense of all of the competing interests for funds and the limitations on satisfying the requesting party's wish. If a devil's advocate is not available, you might read your message aloud and be your own devil's advocate by adopting the requester's perspective. You might ask yourself: how would it feel hearing the denial as it is currently crafted?

❊

Bill, with whom I developed a friendship at the gym, was head of his department at an advertising company. His job included administering and monitoring the budget for his division. One day, one of his team leaders, Sam, approached him with a budget request of nearly $7,500. Sam wished to upgrade to the new version of InDesign, an Adobe software application used to lay out posters, flyers, and other documents. He also wanted to bring in an outside consultant to educate the department on the most efficient way to use InDesign. While Bill valued Sam as a member of his team and a skilled artist, he knew he could not grant the request. Not only were funds very limited, but only a small fraction of the division used InDesign to any extent, and an entire day allocated to learning how to use the program would put his team behind in more time-sensitive work. In addition, the existing edition of InDesign used by the company—while perhaps not as effective as the new one—was adequate for most required tasks.

Bill decided to script out his denial prior to meeting again with Sam to make sure he would not inadvertently offend his employee. When he reviewed by reading aloud the first draft of his script, he realized that he'd focused too much on the utility of the request and might insult Sam's intelligence. Bill needed to treat Sam and his proposal with more deference if he wished to maintain esprit de corps so vital to the success of the company.

So Bill revised his script and was ready for his meeting with Sam. They met in the conference room adjacent to Bill's office. After exchanging pleasantries, Bill looked across the table at Sam and stated:

Sam,

I wish that I could give you better news on your InDesign budget request. While I understand your desire to upgrade, I hope that you can understand the large number of competing requests I receive and the compelling nature of so many. Because of limited resources, I have had to use what funds we have to buttress the needs of the production team. Your department has been so creative in developing ideas that production can't take advantage of them all and utilize them effectively with clients. So we have decided to bring on board additional team members in production—a decision that we believe will benefit us all. Still, I know having a request like yours denied can be frustrating—so can I answer any questions for you?

[Wait for questions if any. When completed, close with the following if appropriate.]

Why don't you keep me posted on what you see as material deficiencies created by the existing InDesign program
that might be resolved by the new edition? And again,
thanks for your good work and leadership.

Sam expressed some disappointment, but appeared to accept
Bill's decision. Bill thought his acquiescence indicated understanding, but he did not receive any requests or ideas regarding
the InDesign program from Sam in the year following the discussion. Despite Sam's lack of communication on the subject,
Bill felt he had done everything he could to make the decision
palatable.

Keep in Mind:

- Rather than a flat refusal, a respectful explanation of the
  denial will go far to maintain motivated team members.
- A cogent rationale for the denial based upon reasons that
  include limited resources, competing interests, and overall
  organizational welfare will help assuage disappointment.
- If no devil's advocate is available, be your own. You can
  read the message aloud and put yourself in the position of
  the listener.

Discharging an Employee Who Is Also Your Friend

Managers sometimes have unique relationships with different
members of their teams. Most, if not all, hopefully fall on the
positive side of the ledger. Some may even lead to close friendships. As a result, a manager may find himself in a bind if he

shares a close bond with one of his charges who is underper-
forming and lacks the ability to improve. It can become awkward
if—after trying to steer the employee to a better track—the manager determines that his friend must be terminated for the good
of the company. The uncomfortable task then requires communicating the termination with the hope of minimal damage to
the personal relationship.

A manager's explanations may not be sufficient to overcome
the employee's hurt feelings and preserve the friendship. But a
script with a clear message may salvage a valued relationship.
The message should express a willingness to give advice as the
terminated employee seeks other opportunities and—assuming
the manager can candidly support it—offer to write the former
employee a recommendation.

No matter what the manager says, the terminated employee
may only hear "termination" and effectively shut down conversation. You might then try to reopen a constructive dialogue
with questions—"Do you understand why I'm saying this?" or
"Do you have any questions?" Questions may help kick-start
dialogue and open channels of communication.

✳

As a teenager, I worked as a lifeguard at a pool in Philadelphia.
One afternoon, I saw a seven-year-old boy and his younger sister
sitting tearfully in the lobby of the swim club. I approached
them and learned that they had just been informed of their dad's
sudden passing due to a heart attack. I took the boy, Ryan, under
my wing that day and for the next five years was his "big brother"
until I left for law school.

Years later, we were reconnected when my law firm's hiring
committee picked him to work in our corporate law department.
Subsequently, due to a consolidation in the department and some

economic changes—as well as his lack of experience in certain specialties for which the firm needed personnel—Ryan had to be terminated. As a result of my close bond with Ryan, I decided that I would communicate to Ryan the firm's decision. As I was jotting down some notes, I knew that I wanted to let Ryan know that, despite the conclusion of his employment, my affection for him continued and to assure him that I would be there for him in the future.

> Ryan,
> Our lives have been intertwined for a number of years. I view our relationship as special and your coming to the firm was a happy occasion for me. So telling you that your work here will have to end soon is not easy for me. The economy and the scope of your practice capabilities dictate that your position will be eliminated. As of sixty days from now, you will no longer be associated with the firm. That is a difficult message for me to deliver to you.
> But I also want you to know that during this remaining period, I and others here will support you as you look for other opportunities and we will also provide you with six months' severance until you find a job in the event your search takes longer than the sixty days.
> I suspect you are overwhelmed by the news. Do you have any questions? [Listen carefully and respond.]
> Please remember, I view you as family, and just as I would tell any of my sons I tell you—when the shock of the decision subsides some, come to me for advice, references, and whatever other support I can give you.
> Is there anything else I can explain? Would you like to have lunch tomorrow after you have had some time to digest this?

Forty-five days following our meeting, Ryan left the firm. He took a job in the corporate law department of an entertainment company. After a decade of hard work, he rose to the top of the company's legal department and then moved to its executive suite. On my desk now sits a plaque commemorating a donation in my name that he and his wife made some years later to support a scholarship for at-risk children.

Keep in Mind:

- Use the two key elements of this situation—acknowledging the importance of your relationship and the finality of the decision—as a guide when scripting this message.
- Devote time practicing delivering the message to reduce discomfort.
- Be prepared for an emotional response and possibly a significant short-term change in your relationship with the former employee.
- Ask questions and express concern to restart the dialogue.
- Allow time for responding or venting.
- Make sure to follow up on that lunch.

Denying a Subordinate's Request for Leave

Most of us are familiar with the stereotype of the tyrannical, inflexible boss, depicted in a plethora of films and television shows, from *Swimming with Sharks* to *Wall Street* to *The Devil's Advocate*, who creates a hostile work environment. These bosses force their employees to work long hours while seemingly breaking their spirits and, at times, the law. Very few leaders want to engender that kind of employee antipathy. But there is a balance

to be struck, because even the best bosses don't want to be push-
overs. There are instances when a manager must firmly say no.
One of these situations arises when an employee's request for a
leave is not supported by company policy or contract. The request might be handled in a variety of ways: from granting the
leave without questioning (being a pushover) to firing the employee for perceived laziness (being a movielike caricature). To
establish a productive and satisfying work setting, the supervisor
must find middle ground that denies the subordinate's request
while maintaining a positive relationship with him.

Many companies offer opportunities for leave for a variety
of reasons. Absent a compelling emergency, the door to a non-
compliant leave request must be closed. The denial should effectively communicate to the employee why the request is being
rejected. The message should avoid personal criticism so as not
to damage the worker's relationship with the company. The employer should consider in advance the range of reactions that a
rejection may provoke in an employee.

❄

Pam, the production manager of one of our law firm's clients, was
approached by her employee, Margaret, with a somewhat unusual
leave request. Margaret stopped by Pam's office one Monday
afternoon and explained that her childhood friend was having a
shotgun wedding that very Thursday. She said her travel would
necessitate taking off Wednesday through Friday. Pam, caught
off guard by the sudden request, told Margaret she would think
it over and get back to her the next day. Hoping to manage
Margaret's expectations, Pam also reminded her of the company
policy that required employees to provide their supervisor with
at least two weeks' notice of any intended absences. Knowing

that the request did not fit the "emergency" leave exception, a denial was in order, so Pam sought time to make some notes and organize her thoughts. Pam valued Margaret as an employee, but she also knew that her absence, even if only for three days, would make it harder to meet production deadlines during the company's busy season and also set a dangerous precedent.

Pam wrote some ideas down quickly, among them expressing her frustration with Margaret's disregard of company policy. When she read it over, Pam recognized that it was too strong.

She needed to erase all language that demonstrated dissatisfaction and simply remind Margaret of the rule in a firm but polite manner. The message Pam communicated to Margaret was straightforward. It said that although Pam wished she could approve the request, she needed all hands on deck this particular week and that the company policy, absent an emergency, could not be waived.

The scripting process completed, Pam stopped by Margaret's workstation the next morning and suggested Margaret join her in her office. Within ten minutes, Margaret was seated across from Pam's desk, filled with visions of flying out the following morning to join her best school friends at the wedding, at which point Pam looked across the desk and delivered her prepared remarks:

> Margaret,
>
> I really am sympathetic and appreciative of your desire to stand by your friend. But I also hope that you are sympathetic to my responsibilities to you and the other people here at the company. You see, we created the policy that requires two weeks' lead time on requests for personal leave in nonemergency situations because of our tight production schedules when orders come in. Well, we are in one of

those periods now and you are essential to helping us successfully execute this customer's order. [Margaret may start to respond at this point. If so, let her speak and get whatever she has off her chest.]

I understand how you feel about this wedding and that you consider it an emergency, but we have been consistent, since the beginning, in considering emergencies to be extraordinary medical or personal need occurrences.

So, Margaret, I cannot grant your leave, but would be happy to consider some time for a trip to visit with your friend and celebrate her marriage next month.

Pam stated her reasons for denying the request while also expressing her appreciation of Margaret's hard work and firmly reminding her of the policy. Although Margaret was disappointed she would miss her friend's wedding, she seemed resigned to Pam's decision. About seven months later, Margaret made another leave request. This time, she was sure to give two weeks' advance notice for leave so she could be at the same friend's baby shower. Pam sent me her story and script after I told her I was working on this book. Her note to me included this assessment: "Scripting has empowered me to be a better manager."

Keep in Mind:

- Keep the language and the tone professional. It is best to communicate in a respectful manner, even if the facts don't warrant it.
- If the employee has not already explained it, ask for the reasoning behind the request so the employee feels he or she is being listened to.

- Give the employee a clear rationale for why the request is being denied.
- Know and explain the repercussions for the company if the employee's leave were granted.
- Offer the employee an alternative course of action that fits the policy.

Offering Constructive Criticism

Dispensing constructive criticism is one of the most important tasks a manager has. But, let's face it, much of the criticism that we offer to business colleagues—and to family and friends—simply doesn't come out as intended. It's often delivered with little forethought and can cause more harm, in the form of bruised feelings, than good.

Presenting criticism constructively is an art. It's not only what you say that's important, it's how you present it. People are often squeamish about delivering negative messages. Their reluctance often causes them to avoid direct criticism—which means they don't do it enough to become accomplished at it.

While every conversation is different, scripting can offer guideposts to make such uncomfortable situations more manageable. Knowing you have the right language to fall back on can embolden you to offer critiques that will be valuable to the targeted employee and organization.

It can be helpful for managers to remember that many people desire feedback. Employees whose job performance is flawed often would prefer a frank conversation with their supervisor—and the chance to improve—before the imperfection erodes their standing within the organization. So giving clear and constructive direction, along with the opportunity to ask questions, enhances the likelihood of these employees elevating their performance.

A newspaper editor once told my writing colleague, Jeff Barker, that his reporters should never be surprised by criticism they receive in their annual performance reviews. Their supervisors, he said, should communicate frankly enough that the staff should be aware of their on-the-job weaknesses—maybe a tendency to miss deadlines, or to not develop sources—by the time they receive their appraisals.

Some people, of course, will resist all but the most positive feedback. But most will take it to heart. "People can do something with the feedback probably 70 percent of the time," Karen May, vice president for people development at Google, told the *New York Times*. "And for the other 30 percent, they are either not willing to take it in, it doesn't fit their self-image, they're too resistant, in denial, or they don't have the wherewithal to change it. And the reality is that most change happens in small increments. So if you're watching to see if someone's changing, you have to watch for the incremental change. It's not a straight line."

✳

Randy had recently begun working as a midlevel editor at a video production firm. Two years out of college, he was younger than most of his colleagues and clients, which included small businesses and nonprofits.

Randy was technically skilled and creative, but his supervisors had detected a problem—he talked incessantly on the job. Randy's excessive chatter—he might talk to coworkers about a movie he had seen or his impending weekend plans—was slowing down work in the editing room. His colleagues were already laboring to meet deadlines editing public-service announcements and other video projects. Randy's talking wasn't conducive to a professional work environment.

Marshall, Randy's immediate supervisor, heard about the problem from some of the other editors. The others felt it would be too awkward to approach Randy themselves about it. They thought the criticism should come from a supervisor.

It was left to Marshall to determine how to approach Randy. He decided to speak to him after their workday ended so that Randy would not be embarrassed in front of his peers. To ease his nerves, Marshall wrote down notes and committed them to memory. It wasn't exactly a script; Marshall had not learned how to script. But it was a rough equivalent that fulfilled the same goals—to make him more confident and prepared for the conversation that followed.

Here is a polished reconstruction of what he wrote:

Randy,
  We like the job you're doing in the editing room. You have a flair for the creative.
  But we believe you can do even better.
  I think you're still getting accustomed to our work culture. As you know, we need to turn around video projects for our clients on tight deadlines.
  This requires speed and teamwork. We believe both of these could be enhanced if you could keep your personal conversations to a minimum.
  [Do you understand what I mean by this?]
  We want to be collegial at the firm. That's why we have our periodic retreats. We're glad you seem to be making friends here.

But we need to keep the larger goals in mind. I know you want to avoid distractions on the job, and talking appears to take your attention—and that of others—off our clients' needs.

I'm happy to discuss this more if you like. Do you have any questions?

After the conversation, Marshall was left with the impression that Randy had no idea he had been talking too much on the job. Probably, Marshall thought, Randy was still transitioning emotionally from a college frat-house atmosphere to a professional job site. He was still learning what constitutes appropriate behavior in the "real world."

The bottom line is that—while Randy remained among the more talkative employees—the number and length of his editing room conversations declined. He seemed to better understand what was expected of him.

Keep in Mind:

- Most workers want to receive feedback even if it is not all positive.
- Be direct and clear about concerns with the employee's conduct.
- The feedback may not take hold immediately but rather over time.
- Focus on the effect the unwanted behavior has on the organization and ask questions to confirm that the employee understands the message.

Turning Down a Job Applicant

Many of us at some point have been turned down for a job. It can be a demoralizing experience. But being the manager who must inform applicants they didn't get the position can be difficult in its own right. Few want to be the bearer of bad news. But there are ways to make the experience more palatable for both parties. And scripting can play an important role in this.

One thing to remember is that turning down a job applicant is not necessarily a disservice. The applicant may simply not be the right fit. Like trying to put a square peg in a round hole, hiring someone for a job for which they are not suited will only end up badly for both parties. Furthermore, months later, the applicant may be hired somewhere else—at a place where they are needed and appreciated. They may then believe it was fortuitous that events unfolded as they did.

The manner in which to deliver the news should vary according to the situation. Consider an applicant who joined hundreds of others in applying for a position online. It is acceptable for an employer to deliver a turndown in the same way the application was received—via an online message.

Candidates who have moved far along in the hiring process, and have been interviewed at least once, merit a different sort of treatment—a letter or phone call. Because it is more personal, a phone call may be preferable in the case of a candidate who wasn't a perfect fit but shows promise for the future. A phone call is also faster, and that's important. The shorter the waiting period, the better. No candidate likes to be kept in limbo. And it's never wise to get into a lengthy discussion with a bitter, unsuccessful candidate, because it can turn personal.

Job applicants should be told—professionally and in concise

language—that their skills aren't the best match for the position. A manager may want to indicate that the candidate's résumé will be kept on hand in case a suitable position comes along.

The best-handled turndowns can be an educational experience. Ideally, the candidate may recognize technical or other skills he or she needs to improve upon to be a better candidate the next time around. The employer should highlight the candidate's strengths and explain that the company's needs were better met by an applicant with different skills or qualifications. Remember to resist the urge to reveal too much about the decision-making process leading to the turndown so as not to open another whole line of inquiry with no intrinsic benefit to either party. The communication should be cordial, respectful, and—most important—to the point.

⁕

John, a friend of my writing partner Jeff Barker, was a high-ranking manager of a nonprofit environmental organization based in Washington. As the head of development, it fell on him to hire a new fund-raiser.

The organization had winnowed a list of dozens of candidates down to two finalists. Both had good "people" skills—they could be charming to potential donors and work well with their colleagues at the nonprofit. But one was clearly superior. He was more experienced generally and more acclimated to the landscape—the foundations and corporations that had been willing to make significant donations in the past. The other candidate, Jeremy, had a liability. He was not a skilled writer. The sample direct-mail appeals and grant applications he submitted lacked polish, and some contained grammatical errors.

John knew that Jeremy—whom he had interviewed several

days earlier—would be let down by not getting the job. Always eager to please, John felt uncomfortable delivering disappointing news. He considered having to reject job candidates among the worst of all office tasks.

Once, he had turned down a job candidate who continued to question him—belittle him, even—over why he had not been offered the position. John had held his ground, keeping his responses short. But it had been an unpleasant experience for John.

This time, John decided to jot down some rough notes to ease his anxiety—a script of sorts. And before finalizing them, he spoke them out loud to himself—he was his own devil's advocate. His notes looked something like this:

Jeremy,
This is John from [the nonprofit]. I'm calling about the fund-raising position you applied for.

We enjoyed meeting with you, and we liked hearing your thoughts about the position.

After speaking with you, we think you would have brought lots of positives to our organization, but we went with somebody whose qualifications we believe are a better match for the job. This person's experience in grant writing and direct-mail campaigns gave him the edge.

One thing we noticed—and were impressed with—is that you have a friendly, easy manner that seems suitable for the sort of informal contacts people in our profession must make at receptions, conferences, and other events. That, combined with building your other skills, will take you a long way in this field.

We hope you will keep in touch and we plan to keep your résumé on file in case another position opens up that matches your skills. Do you have any questions?

We appreciate your interest in us, and we wish you the best of luck.

Having his notes in hand allowed John to relax during the phone call. Because it was not a face-to-face meeting, John found himself reading sections of the script verbatim to Jeremy to make certain his words were correctly parsed.

Jeremy was cordial. The only time John had to deviate from the script was when Jeremy politely asked what he might do to bolster his credentials.

This gave John an opening to mention the writing. "I'd keep writing those sample fund-raising appeals," John told Jeremy diplomatically. "Polish them, hone them, and show them to people in the business—even just your friends—to get input on good writing and what works and what doesn't." Jeremy expressed his thanks, and John moved on with his next task.

Keep in Mind:

- Keep the turndown professional. Don't allow it to lapse into a personal conversation.
- Resist the urge to reveal too much about the inner workings of the decision-making process leading to the turndown. That should remain private.
- Provide an explanation that can help the candidate going forward.
- Tailor the medium of the turndown—e-mail, letter, or phone call—to the seriousness of the job candidate's prospects and to the level of contact with the employer to that point.
- Don't keep the candidate waiting for a verdict any longer than necessary.

CHAPTER 7

❊

Problems Employees Face

Inquiring about Your Status following a Job Interview

Have you ever left a job interview both anxious to hear the employer's decision and worried about the result: getting the job? The hiring process can drag on for days or even weeks and as time goes by, your anxiety level rises.

This feeling can be alleviated by reaching out to the interviewer in hopes of obtaining information or at least staying in the mind of the potential employer. A new concern, however, then arises: what to say or how to say it? Generally, it is useful to offer an expression of gratitude along with an offer to respond to any lingering questions. A request regarding the timing of the decision should conclude the inquiry.

In some cases, the script may not be designed for an oral conversation. It may take the form of an e-mail or letter that reminds the prospective employer of you while not making you seem overly aggressive or a pest. Requesting another

in-person interview could be viewed as overreaching by the
other party.

❋

My associate's daughter-in-law, Nicole, a rising young executive
seeking a new job, encountered this scenario a few years ago
after she interviewed with a rapidly growing international transportation company. At the suggestion of a friend who held a
seat on the company's advisory board, Nicole had applied for a
high-level role focused on developing strategic partnerships.
Although she had other job offers in hand, she felt this job, more
than any other, put her in a cutting-edge industry with endless
opportunities for growth. Nicole initially interviewed with the
company's hiring partner, Steve, and believed their meeting
"went great." She built a good rapport with Steve and was
informed that she would be brought back for a second interview
with other members of the company's leadership team.

The second interview took place a week later. Nicole met with
the president and CEO, the chief technology officer, the chief
marketing executive, and Steve. After a three-and-a-half-hour interview process, Nicole left feeling even more confident about the
impression she made. She answered all of their questions directly
and saw positive signs in their facial expressions. As she was de-
parting, Steve again praised her but also remarked that one or
more of the interviewers had expressed the concern that, based on
her résumé, Nicole "may lack" real, applied experience driving
strategic partnerships through the nuts and bolts of the deal process. Later that day, Nicole received an e-mail from Steve informing her that the company was impressed with her background in
negotiating deals and that he hoped to get back to her "in the next
couple of weeks" regarding their decision.

After a few weeks passed with no news, Nicole was anxious to receive a sense of her status, but did not want her inquiry to sound too aggressive. Her second-choice opportunity had given her another two weeks to make a decision. Consequently, I advised her to script out an e-mail inquiry. Nicole's script represented a balancing act of sorts. Since she was seeking a deal-making position, she pondered whether the situation called for an "outright ask" for the position to demonstrate her strength as a deal maker. Her ultimate goal was to allay the concerns Steve had expressed and to obtain a sense of where she stood while sustaining the group's interest in her. After some further discussion with me, Nicole abandoned the "outright ask" approach. Instead, she included an expression of gratitude coupled with an offer to answer any questions that may have arisen and furnished additional information to address other concerns that had been raised. She also wanted to have a clear sense of the timing of their decision. The timing was important because of the two-week window she had for accepting the other job opportunity. She was armed with information she had received from her advisory board friend that the field of candidates had been narrowed to Nicole and another person. She then scripted her interview follow-up e-mail.

Dear Steve,

This is just a quick note to touch base as I understand that it may be a week or so before I hear back from you.

As I continue to learn about [name of the company], my interest and enthusiasm grows. After our meeting I connected with my friend [name of the friend], who has been following the company for the last year. She reaffirmed my feelings going in—that the company has great growth potential and the team necessary to help it become the force that you project.

I also thought about the mention you made about my experience level in executing strategic partnership deals. The attached page will provide you and the interview committee some further insight into my experience in that area. If any questions remain on that subject or any other matter relating to my qualifications, please do not hesitate to contact me.

As you know, I am exploring several other opportunities and hope that I will hear something back from you in the next two weeks. Is this a reasonable time estimate? Thanks again for the opportunity to meet with you all and for your guidance.

One week later, Nicole got a response to her e-mail with good news. She received the job, and Steve and his associates have never regretted having her as a key member of their team. In the past two years, she has helped the company build partnerships throughout the world. I recently saw Nicole at a nonprofit event in Boston and got a big hug. She also told me how scripting now plays a major role in her deal presentations.

Keep in Mind:

- Some conversations are better conducted through e-mail rather than in person, particularly follow-ups.
- If you have a deadline on another job offer, you may have to set a certain date for a decision. Be careful not to make it a demand, but rather something that arises out of not wanting to miss the opportunity to work for the company.
- You may sense resistance to your need to hear back. Seek a coach or adviser to help you pace yourself and keep things in perspective.

- Address any concerns you believe the other party may have about you in a nondefensive manner.

Asking for a Raise

How often does someone feel they deserve a raise, plan to ask for it, and then slink away in retreat? Or make the request, and then, when speaking, reduce the demand for fear of being rejected? Or go in with guns blazing and put off the other side? All too frequently, a lack of confidence and experience in negotiating creates a disappointing impact. Feeling overworked and underpaid can deteriorate your work ethic and positive attitude. Asking for a raise—while difficult and uncomfortable—can, under the right circumstances, make you more productive and satisfied.

The key is to have a certain detachment. It's best to state the case for a raise unemotionally and methodically, employing as many facts as possible. It's appropriate to cite specific accomplishments, extra hours worked, and, if you know them, some comparables—the salaries of others in your position who are making more money. It's wise to ask for a little more than you expect. This is, after all, a negotiation.

⁎

I remember the case of my friend Fred. After leading a series of successful marketing campaigns for his company, Fred felt that his annual 3 percent salary increase was both inadequate and an affront. Although his compensation package was satisfactory when he joined the company's marketing team, it quickly became clear that he was the creative leader. Yet he was making $110,000 per year while several other comparable midlevel executives in his department were earning at least $150,000. Adding to his agitation was the significant increase in his workload during the past several years since he was the go-to guy on key campaigns requiring creativity.

By the time Fred came to me for advice, his disappointment had reached a level that had him considering unloading his frustrations on his manager with a personal attack about being treated "unfairly" and "taken advantage of." His approach was not a case of retreat, but rather a full-scale assault—without any hint of diplomacy—on the citadel of executive decision making. He was prepared to charge into his manager's office with a set of emotional demands. As Fred vented, I could only think of the words of the writer Ambrose Bierce: "Speak when you are angry, and you will make the best speech you will ever regret."

I explained to Fred, just as I would to someone too timid to ask for an adequate raise, the process of scripting. He assented to employing the scripting process before making the ask. We worked on how to confidently present his case without making it personal. The script we ultimately crafted could apply with equal force to support the request if one were hesitant or emotional.

> I am very pleased that I have had the opportunity to have an impact on this business. At the same time, I've done some thinking about my role, what I have accomplished, and the scope of my duties. I am working extraordinarily hard—for example, I designed and led three major marketing campaigns in the last eight months and at least that many in prior periods. As I look back on my job description and my current workload, it's apparent that my workload and impact exceed what was expected when I took this job.
>
> [If it feels appropriate you may ask: "How do you view my performance?" or "Do you agree?"]

In light of the compensation packages of others in comparable positions to mine, and even more important the creative impact I have had, the tremendous jump in workload, and my willingness to assist and guide others, my annual compensation should be increased to $160,000 per annum.* I hope you agree and that this terrific relationship can go forward with both of us feeling good about it.

* Fred asked for $10,000 more than the comparables to satisfy the negotiation principle "aim high but with reason."

Confident in his presentation, Fred got his boss's attention, but not an immediate response. Despite his strong feelings, he began to wonder whether he had asked for too much. Imagine then the smile that came over his face when, five days later, he was called into his manager's office and informed that, starting the next month, his compensation would be raised to $150,000 per year.

Keep in Mind:

- Tailor the script to the special circumstances of your job and compensation history.
- Be prepared for silence or a negative response—don't go into retreat because of the listener's reaction. Just say: "I would appreciate it if you would give this some further thought," or if you get a push-back in the response, ask: "Could you tell me what you mean by that?"
- Aim high with reason. Even if you want to tell the employer your bottom line, leave yourself some room.
- Be ready with questions regarding concerns your employer may express.
- Speak with confidence, but not antagonistically. In this case it's both what you say and how you say it that matter.

Confronting Sexual Harassment

One goes through countless interactions in a typical business day. We ride the elevator with fellow employees, pass their desks on our way to the printer, work on group projects together, and engage in constant communication. These interactions can occasionally turn unprofessional or predatory. Perhaps a coworker touches another employee, makes suggestive comments relating to appearance, or e-mails images that border on inappropriateness. All of these actions, ranging from minor to severe, are examples of sexual harassment and can cause the harassed employee, and possibly those around him or her, to become increasingly uncomfortable.

Sexual harassment is a difficult and sensitive topic for anyone to confess to another. The embarrassment often felt from reporting the behavior can be a tough obstacle to overcome. Yet it should not be taken lightly. The offensive action has the power to affect its targets' psychological mind-set, physical health, and multiple areas in their careers. If not confronted, the behavior will continue because ignoring it is often perceived by the aggressor as agreement or encouragement.

While communicating the concern to human resources in companies large enough to have such a department may be a first step, it is important to consult legal counsel at the outset. If counsel agrees, the sexual harassment victim should communicate a strong message of protest to the aggressor. Prepare for the conversation by writing down feelings to increase the possibility of maintaining composure when confronting the offender. It is also beneficial to gather support for legal claims by saving text messages, printing e-mails, and preserving recollections of anyone witnessing an interaction. Review the employee handbook to see if someone is designated to assist in the situation. The message should not be vague. State clearly what the harasser has done and firmly explain that it must stop.

※

Karen, a dental hygienist, worked in a private dentistry group in Washington, DC. Until six months ago, she was content with her job. Although her salary was fair and her career path promising, she was growing increasingly uncomfortable around Lloyd, the dentist in the office with whom she interacted the most. What began as playful comments about her resembling a model turned into Lloyd asking her out for drinks and making crude jokes. Her fellow hygienists were also aware of Lloyd's "special" treatment—some were uncomfortable with it while others made snide comments about her professionalism. Karen hoped that if she ignored Lloyd's behavior, he would grow bored and stop.

Instead, Lloyd took her silence as a sign of approval. For the next two months, Karen was subjected to unwanted touching and bumping in the hallway. Even when she was with patients, Lloyd would enter the room and press his body against hers while working on patients. Karen did not want to embarrass him by telling him to stop in front of the patients, and by the time they left the exam room, she would lose her nerve to say anything. She needed her job and feared she might put it at risk by standing up to him.

At the suggestion of her sister, who had been a student at a bar review I taught, Karen called me for some legal guidance. With the help of a partner in my law firm, I was able to convey to Karen her legal rights. I also learned that if there was a way to get him to stop without resorting to litigation, she would prefer to go that route.

I coached her for her meeting with Lloyd by taking her through a specific course of action. Initially I asked her to send me a draft of a letter to him expressing her feelings about what he was doing and demanding that he stop before she had to take some form of legal action. I also advised that she inform him that if he ended the offensive behavior, they could hopefully continue a professional relationship without causing further distress or damaging his reputation. I promised her that the letter was just an exercise and would not be sent. Karen wrote several iterations of the message. I instructed her to turn the final one into a script, which she carefully practiced and ultimately delivered to Lloyd in the employee break room, which was adjacent to the reception area and had doors on both sides. Her script started with this note to herself:

[Compose myself as best I can before I say this, and if he should become offensive or push back too hard, tell him that he will hear from my lawyer and walk out. Most important, deliver the message in a place where I can easily access an exit to avoid him physically blocking me in.]

Lloyd,
You've hurt me very badly. If the comments about my appearance and being hit on aren't offensive enough, your touching me certainly is. The way you touch and rub up against me has caused me great emotional distress. While I thought the first time it happened was just a mistake, your persistence in doing it and your repeated conduct has caused me to see a lawyer. I have gathered evidence from statements by other people in the office and recorded some offensive statements you've said as you touched me.
This conversation is not about my wanting to sue you, but just about asking you to stop touching me as we work

together or in any other contexts. If you don't stop, I will take action and I have promised my lawyer that I will check in with him every two weeks to confirm to him that no further unwanted touching by you or uncomfortable comments have occurred.

When Lloyd reacted defensively and angrily toward what Karen said, she repeated a scripted contingency for that reaction:

If you want to get angry, then I suggest you go see your lawyer because I will be going to see mine. If, however, you agree to stop and in fact stop, then we will move forward as I've stated.

Lloyd paused to collect himself. He flatly apologized for upsetting her and promised to be nothing less than formal. I am happy to report that during all of our check-in calls the following six months, Lloyd was no longer bothering her and she was once again content with her job.

Keep in Mind:

- With the advice of counsel, if necessary, script out and deliver your message sooner rather than later. The longer you allow the sexual harassment to continue, the more it may appear that you are comfortable with the behavior.
- Try not to be emotional when you script. Approach the discussion calmly and with clear and definitive statements.
- Practice with a supportive friend to reduce any feelings of apprehension you may have about the delivery.

Disputing a Negative Evaluation—a Script Serves
a Dual Purpose

Just when you've outgrown report cards, along comes the equivalent for grown-ups: performance reviews. Performance reviews can provoke the same sort of angst from employees that report cards once elicited in students. You're being evaluated—judged. You want to do well and be assessed fairly.

But how do you handle it when you receive a negative performance review—particularly one you feel is unwarranted? This isn't grade school anymore. The ability to prepare a rebuttal effectively could hold consequences for your future employment—as well as your own morale. It's important to stick up for yourself—but to do it in a professional manner that doesn't alienate your bosses and get you branded as a whiner. That can be a delicate balancing act.

Many performance evaluations are followed by meetings with your supervisor. A script can help guide you through these sessions, providing talking points in face-to-face meetings. But carefully scripted thoughts can do more. They can help you prepare a rebuttal that explains your perspective, to be included in your employee file. Your file should contain a written response to the critical review—even if one isn't required. A written response captures your arguments and preserves them for anyone who may read the review down the line. "You need a written record of your dissent," says Bill O'Brien, a partner at Miller O'Brien Jensen, an employment law firm in Minneapolis. "Without it, if the situation advances to the point of litigation, you've essentially got no ground to stand on."

The response should be specific and well documented. Relying on facts—how you resolved a client's complaint or that you

stayed late to complete a fund-raising appeal—will help you resist the impulse to delve into personal attacks on your evaluator.
You are making a reasoned argument—as if appealing a court
verdict. You don't need to detail all you've done for the company
or highlight your meritorious qualities. This isn't a job interview. Rather, it's best to focus as specifically as possible on how
the negative review could be more accurate. Consider that the
supervisor may have missed something about you, not that he or
she was operating in bad faith. Verbally attacking your boss's
judgment won't help you achieve your objectives.

The best reviews won't contain big surprises. Good managers
communicate with their workers sufficiently enough that the employees usually know what their manager considers their short-
comings well before the formal evaluation is presented. Sometimes
supervisors overlook things. Your job is to complete the record—
to fill in the blanks about who you are and what you've done.

You also may need to acknowledge that some of the criticism
may genuinely be constructive. Supervisors aren't inclined to
give perfect reviews. Almost all employees have performance
traits they can improve on. It's best to show a willingness to improve and to accept that you're not always going to emerge with
"straight As."

✳

Don was a staff writer for an online business news website. After
eight years of employment, he had established a solid record of
seeking out and writing polished, accurate stories.

Don also had what he considered a security blanket: his immediate supervisor, Brian, was a midlevel editor who seemed to
appreciate Don's work. It helped that Don felt a natural connection with Brian. Both were originally from the New York City

area and were Yankees fans. When they met in the morning, they often rehashed the previous night's game or generally talked baseball.

But midway through the year, Don learned through a companywide e-mail that Brian was leaving to accept a post at a competing website. Brian was replaced by a senior reporter whom Don barely knew. Don hadn't known Brian was leaving, and he knew he faced an adjustment working without him, but he soon settled back into his routine. He continued to produce three to four stories a week. On Tuesday and Thursday mornings, Don also still made sure he got to work before nine because those were the days he needed to leave early to pick up his second-grade son from after-school activities. Unlike before, however, Don now was also asked to edit some of the other writers' work. Don didn't think much about his performance review until it arrived in March. The review described Don as proficient and experienced. He was surprised, however, by some of the other language. It said Don had been slow to adequately embrace his new responsibilities—the editing. It also questioned whether his work hours were suitable for the needs of the website, suggesting Don should show more "flexibility."

Don was initially angered by the review. He couldn't help but wonder if Rich, his new boss, felt threatened or insecure by the close working relationship that Don had previously enjoyed with Brian. He also considered whether Rich might be trying to establish his authority by writing a tougher-than-warranted initial evaluation.

Don decided to draft a written response to the evaluation to be saved in his employee file. In his message he didn't hint at any of his theories about Rich because they were merely supposition and far too personal to become part of a company dialogue. Don used his letter and adapted it into a script he planned to use during his evaluation conference with his new boss to feel more confident and refrain from saying anything he would later regret.

Rich,

   Thank you for your evaluation. I've read it carefully and I appreciate your comments about my writing proficiency. I've always considered my writing to be a strength.

   I wonder if we could discuss your comments about my not "fully embracing" my new editing responsibilities. This was a new assignment, but one I was happy to take on—particularly if I could help along some of the younger writers who are still learning the fundamentals of the craft. Have you talked to some of those younger writers [mention two by name whose editing experiences have been favorable] to ask them whether the editing sessions have been useful for them?

   If there is anything in my editing that needs to be corrected, I would be happy to make accommodations. Is there something you saw that concerned you?

   I would also be happy to talk about flexibility in my hours. I should have done a better job of explaining my Tuesday-Thursday schedule. It really is more flexible than it seems. My second-grader has to be picked up at the bus on those days, but I can usually get a neighbor or babysitter to fill in if there is an important work issue that day. I did that on [cite dates] when I had to stay late because of the companywide computer issues.

   I appreciate your talking this through with me. I think we share the same goals for the direction we want the site to go. By the way, would you put this written summary of my concerns in my file?

Don's session with Rich was cordial, if not friendly. Rich expressed his concerns that Don was too rigid in his editing and that some of the younger writers felt he was sometimes short with them. He also acknowledged that Don's tough approach worked well for some writers, but asked that he show more patience with others. Rich did modify the language in the review about Don's inflexible work hours. He said he better understood that Don was doing the best he could to meet the site's needs.

Keep in Mind:

- Always offer a written response to the evaluation even if one is not requested. Use the written script as the basis for your oral discussion.
- Find common ground with the supervisor—perhaps in shared company goals or approaches.
- Be as specific as possible in your rebuttal; keep the discussion focused on ways you have done your job that may not have been immediately evident.
- Be willing to accept criticism that is genuinely constructive.
- Politely request that a copy of your letter or written summary of your account go in your file.

Dealing with a Boss Who Is a Bully

If you've ever experienced a bullying boss, you can take comfort in knowing you're not alone. All too many of us have encountered screaming bosses, browbeating bosses, or manipulative bosses.

In my 2005 book *Bullies, Tyrants, and Impossible People*, I devoted an entire chapter to "the boss from hell." I outlined a boss of the worst sort—someone who is "clearly, plainly, absolutely, totally, off-the-charts, without exception, all-the-time, over-the-top difficult."

There are no remedies for some of these bosses. And it can be difficult to fight back, even if you have access to a human resources person to whom your grievance might be addressed. "Subordinates know viscerally the high cost of going around a boss, even if it is simply to file a complaint with the human resources department," the *New York Times* wrote in 2004. "You are trouble. You are a whiner. You have called out the manager behind his back." But it's always worth trying to improve your situation.

The first step is realizing you are not powerless, especially if you are contributing to your organization in a meaningful way. You have value to your firm by virtue of your talents and experience.

And you usually have the option to leave. I'm reminded of the old story—often repeated on Capitol Hill and in the media— of the U.S. Senate aide who was said to depart with a message to the boss saying: "Life is too precious to spend another minute of it with you."

If you make a confident enough presentation that seems important and heartfelt, even if your boss is a screamer, he is likely to listen. Be prepared, however, to let him shout without taking it personally. Neutralizing your emotions is a prerequisite to exchanges with difficult people. The key is not to be passive. There are acceptable ways to stand up for yourself so you're no longer somebody's punching bag.

A script will help to frame the issue in a way the boss can understand. A good strategy is to talk specifically about how the bullying hurts productivity and morale. Putting the bullying into such concrete terms makes it less of a personal issue and more of a work issue.

※

A friend of mine, Jake, was a midlevel executive at a public relations firm. He routinely had two or three clients, usually trade associations, which he expertly juggled. He got along well with the clients. That wasn't the problem. It was his boss.

On Sunday evenings at his home—usually just after dinner— Jake would begin to feel edgy. His stomach would begin to bother him, and he sometimes had trouble falling asleep at night.

Jake was barely aware of this Sunday pattern until one day he realized that it was a reaction to the prospect of dealing with his difficult boss for another workweek. Jake had been internalizing his anxiety until it practically made him sick.

Jake's boss, Frank, didn't communicate well. He seemed fond of doling out criticism; he often accused Jake of not spending enough time cultivating new clients. He didn't seem interested in hearing Jake's rebuttals. Jake and other workers at the firm began to refer to Frank privately as a "one-way transmitter." But it wasn't Frank's poor communication skills that most disturbed Jake. It was the yelling.

Frank was a screamer—a bully. It was hard to predict when he would go off. Each morning, Jake and his colleagues would try to gauge what sort of mood Frank was in. If Frank appeared stressed—perhaps there was an unhappy client or he was having difficulties at home—the employees would do their best to steer clear of the boss. Nobody wanted a confrontation.

Jake often fretted in advance about upcoming conversations with Frank. More than a few times, Frank had raised his voice unexpectedly to berate Jake over his handling of a work issue. To

Jake, Frank's tone often appeared condescending—as if Frank were lecturing a child.

These conversations lingered with Jake, sapping him of his enthusiasm for his job. Jake considered Frank's tone inappropriate and unprofessional.

After soliciting advice from friends, Jake followed a variation of the three Ds (Draft, Devil's Advocate, and Deliver).

The first thing he did—before drafting a brief message to deliver to his boss—was to vent. He imagined what he *might* say, what he wanted to say.

> You are a bully. If you want your employees to take initiative and act like adults, then you need to stop treating us like children.

Of course Jake didn't really say that. But venting it helped him to allow his feelings to bubble to the surface.

Jake also considered leaving the firm. But there were too many aspects of the job that he liked—his peers, his clients, his salary.

Instead, Jake decided to address the matter directly with Frank. Now he had to decide when and how to do it.

Jake decided to wait for an opportune time to speak to Frank about his bullying. Rather than approaching the subject cold, Jake would wait until a moment when Frank was in prime bullying mode. He would, in effect, catch Frank in the act and then—delicately—address Frank's behavior.

In the script he had drafted and practiced with friends, Jake was clear about his concerns without seeming accusatory.

> I wonder if we could stop here for a moment. I'm not quite comfortable when the conversation heats up this way. Is it okay if we cool things down a little bit?

I think we have shared goals on this—and I think I'd function better having a different sort of tone.

I just want to make sure I understand what you want and that we're really communicating . . .

[wait for response]

Since he didn't know how the conversation would unfold, Jake added a note at the top of his script to guide him:

[Don't back down, but don't make it personal. Say what you need to say about the tone and then move the discussion back to work topics. This is, after all, about a business matter.]

Jake also crafted a second script to be used in the event that his initial message was received poorly. In this second script, Jake planned to say—forthrightly—that he would be prepared to leave.

I hope we're able to work this out. If we're not, then I'm not sure that I'd be comfortable continuing at the firm. I think I bring a lot to my job, and I hope I can remain. But if you feel the need to communicate with me this way, maybe I should move on.

Jake didn't need to resort to the second script. His initial script seemed to help his situation, but not immediately. The first time he launched into the message, there was a long pause from Frank. It was as if the boss didn't quite know what to make of his employee's concern.

Over time, however, Frank seemed to be a little more cautious about losing his temper with Jake and did tone down his occasional outbursts. Frank seemed to tread more lightly—a result that Jake considered a satisfactory result. Jake also tempered his expectations. In the past, he seemed to go into every encounter with his boss anticipating that, this time, things would proceed smoothly.

A friend gave him some advice: "You can't go into the same situation each time and expect a different result."

Now he was more realistic. He accepted that he had a difficult boss, and he was better prepared to handle it. It made him feel empowered that he had been able to raise the bullying issue with his boss in a direct way and that at least he was dealing with less of a bully.

Keep in Mind:

- You often have more leverage than you think. You are not powerless.
- Sometimes the best time to point out objectionable behavior is right when it is happening.
- Steer clear of personal attacks. This is about business.
- Not every situation is fixable. In such a case it may be best to find a new job.
- Be clear about the effect that the bullying is having on morale and your job performance.

Obtaining Help to Curtail a Coworker's Personal Attacks

Reputation serves as the filter through which an individual is perceived and it frequently affects how one is treated. A person's social identity is the result of an unspoken evaluation of decisions and actions. From clothes worn to school attended, from professional pursuits to the friends one acquires, an image is created and reinforced. Although it may take years to build a positive reputation, a single misguided action can permanently damage it. A tarnished reputation not only affects one's personal life, but also extends into the professional world. Consider how gossip or malicious comments in the workplace can damage a reputation and sidetrack a career path. Whether true or not, comments made about one's psychological well-being, inappropriate relationship with a coworker, lack of effort on a project, or tendency to push work onto others have the power to spin out of control and ruin a career.

Whether articulated to a friendly manager or taken to human resources personnel in a larger company, responding quickly to false accusations or rumors may be necessary to stem the tide that could drown a career. The scripting process can assist in fashioning a response that saves a job or other relationships and puts an end to scurrilous accusations. The message delivered needs to accomplish more than simply creating a "he said, she said" situation. It needs to convey a reasonable basis for questioning the attacker and for supporting the potential consequences, such as the resignation of the attacked employee or legal action.

✳

Two years ago Robin, after working as a bookkeeper elsewhere, returned to work as a bookkeeper at a company where she'd been before and for the first eighteen months was content with the job. For the most part, she had a positive relationship with her coworkers and superiors; but Mary, the office administrator, was an exception. Although she could not recall ever offending Mary, Robin became aware that Mary had felt animosity toward Robin ever since she'd returned to the company and, worse, Mary had recently begun spreading accusations. Mary was telling others that Robin was failing to fulfill her thirty-five-hour-a-week commitment and taking time from her job to perform part-time work elsewhere—causing Mary to have to pick up some of Robin's hours. In reality, the exact opposite was true. It was Mary who was consistently absent and delegating her responsibilities to others. To make the situation worse, a confidant informed Robin that she'd overheard Mary making other false claims about Robin to one of the partners. Robin knew that this would not be Mary's last attack on her reputation and feared this slander might lead to an unjust termination.

After discussing the predicament, I suggested Robin write her thoughts down to make her case to Hank, a friend at work who was a high-level partner, in order to assuage her fears and frustrations. It took several drafts, but we settled on the following e-mail.

Hank,

Normally I would not write a note like this but instead talk to you directly. Nevertheless I am so upset, both because of the untruths that have been told about me and the fact that they seem to have been taken seriously by some people, that I must write to keep my emotions in check.

You are my friend and confidant. I never thought that I'd come back to [the company], but I came back in large part because of my relationship with you and your role as a future leader of the company. I never suspected at the time I returned that I would grow to care so much about the company as I do now. And I genuinely continue to appreciate your support.

Despite the issues with Mary (not of my own doing, mind you), the experience has been wonderful. I enjoy working at [the company] and being supportive of its future, and the last two years have flown by. My goal has always been to stick around until you take over as managing partner, at which time there might be the opportunity for me to play a more meaningful role.

But now I wonder if it's worth staying around a place where someone can speak such untruths and perpetrate lies and still have credibility. What Mary has said about me has shaken me and I'm seriously considering whether I should remain. Rest assured my commitment has been such that I have been willing to work as hard as required to support [the company].

And I know in my heart that if I do leave, no replacement will care as much and do the job I do. I bring an uncommon level of commitment, energy, calming demeanor, and affection for the company, much more so than my untruthful critic. Up to this point, I have kept my powder dry, but the total perversion of the truth recently put out there makes me wonder whether it is worth carrying on.

I genuinely appreciate and value your support and counsel and therefore now need to ask: What do you think I should do? I look forward to your thoughts.

Although Robin was nervous how Hank would react to her e-mail, she was relieved to have finally confronted Mary's slanders and expressed her frustration. The next morning, she received the following e-mail from Hank:

Robin,

I cannot tell you how much I appreciate your influence in the office, and trust me I completely understand your frustration and appreciate what you are going through. Hopefully you are in today and we can spend a few minutes talking about this . . . I have a few thoughts. Hank

Robin was reassured by Hank's response. It meant a lot to her that he supported her. When she walked into Hank's office later that afternoon, Robin was greeted by Hank and two other partners—a majority of the management committee. They informed her to "just keep doing what you do best . . . keep your head down and work away. You are so much needed here now and in the future." Five months later, Hank was managing partner and Robin, still at the company, happily moved into a new and larger office. Mary no longer worried or threatened her in any manner.

Keep in Mind:

- Find someone to talk to—so you do not let your hurt feelings erupt into precipitous action. And use this person as a coach and ally.
- Declare the truth, but recognize it could be your word against theirs. Save supporting evidence where possible.
- Chronicle incidents and events if possible so you have a paper trail.
- A written message may help you make a contemporaneous record of your position should you have to resort to legal action.

CHAPTER 8

✳

Media Matters

Avoiding the Ill-Advised Tweet

There is something irresistible about tweeting. The speed and immediacy can be alluring, particularly to young people. You can communicate—to multiple audiences—almost as quickly as still-developing thoughts arrive in your brain. And that's where people create problems for themselves—with those pesky, unformed thoughts. On Twitter, all messages come out the same—as 140-character-or-less bursts. A random observation may look the same to the recipient as a Shakespearean gem of profound wisdom. But there are no rewrites or do-overs. Once a tweet has been sent, it is as irrevocable as a fallen snowflake.

Texting potentially comes with many of the same pitfalls. It may have a more intimate feel than tweeting because it is usually between just two people. But don't be lulled into a false sense of security: once you send a text, you can't be certain who will see it. Many of the guidelines in this chapter apply equally to tweeting and texting. Social media differs from personal contact. In conversation, there is context. Two people chatting over dinner assess each other's expressions, tone, and demeanor. It's easier in person to gauge when a comment is intended as a joke. Tweets are more tone-deaf.

And then there is this critical difference: when you're speaking to someone in person, you know exactly who you're talking to. In a restaurant, you may lower your voice so as not to be overheard. There is no such safeguard in tweeting. Your messages can be endlessly retweeted, copied, and otherwise recirculated. We are accountable for our tweets, no matter who reads them. That's why preparation matters. The technology may be speedy, but our use of it can still be well reasoned.

While a full-blown script may not be practical or desirable, working through a draft of sorts—if only on sensitive topics—will ensure that the tweeter thinks before he tweets.

If the tweet is going to address a delicate political or social issue—or opine on the work or character of another, or on a product or service—you may want to write out your proposed thoughts before pulling the Twitter trigger. You may then have a friend or associate critique your thought before it is launched into the social media sphere.

The tweet may be brief, but what it says can have enduring impact.

❈

It was a Saturday afternoon in February, and Terrell Stoglin was frustrated. The University of Maryland basketball guard—the leading scorer in the Atlantic Coast Conference—was having a bad game against Duke, and so was his team. Maryland was losing in the second half at Duke's Cameron Indoor Stadium, and Stoglin found himself slouching on the bench after his shot selection was questioned by his coach.

Stoglin took to Twitter to vent. After the game, reporters covering the team noticed a sarcastic tweet on Stoglin's account noting how much he "loved" sitting on the bench. Predictably, Stoglin's tweet—seeming to publicly question his coach's decision to remove him from the game—was widely retweeted. Within hours of the game, Maryland athletic officials were being asked about the player's tweet and overall conduct.

Soon came another tweet from the player: "Never tweet after a loss. not a bad dude just frustrated. Love terpnation! My fault." The next month, Stoglin told the *Baltimore Sun*: "At the point I was tweeting, I wasn't thinking at all."

Stoglin is far from the first person, of course, to have experienced a disconnect between thinking and tweeting. Former U.S. Representative Anthony Weiner tweeted photos of his private parts covered only by underwear. A Chrysler contractor tweeted an expletive in an unflattering message about the city of Detroit and lost the account and his job.

Imagine how different the outcomes might have been if they'd asked themselves basic guideline questions like the following:

- Is my tweet appropriate for a wide audience? Who is it that I am actually intending to communicate with, and should I, instead, do it in such a way—a meeting or phone call—that will probably remain private?
- Who am I representing in my tweet [or text]? Am I sending from a business account? If so, I might seem to be speaking for my employer instead of only for myself.

- Are my words precise enough, or did I leave them so vague that they could be misinterpreted, particularly by people who don't know me?
- Do I completely understand the technology? Do I understand the difference between sending a direct Twitter message and replying to a tweet in a way that all of the other person's followers can see?
- Should someone else read this before I send it?

Keep in Mind:

- Think before you tweet or text.
- Understand that you may be held accountable for your messages.
- Don't forget that your audience may be wider than you imagine.
- If it has the potential to be misinterpreted or seen as controversial, share it with a devil's advocate first.

Preparing for a Media Interview

There are so many ways to get "on the air" these days. The proliferation of cable stations, talk radio shows, and Internet sites and programming has created new opportunities for aspiring media professionals—and everybody else. "You're not anybody in America unless you're on TV," says Nicole Kidman's lead character in *To Die For.*

But what if you are summoned for a broadcast interview— say, as an expert in your field or the subject of a news profile— and are reluctant to appear?

You may be worried about the amount of exposure. Or about the format. It can be uncomfortable ceding control of an interview to a television or radio anchor or talk show host you have never met. That can be a leap of faith. Or you may be anxious about the interview being broadcast live.

It turns out the preparation required to be a compelling interviewee is similar to what media professionals do themselves before going live. It's about knowing your topic well enough to find your comfort zone. So to start, consider whether you should do some research to add to your existing knowledge of the interview subject. Then get your thoughts down on paper or your computer screen and share them with your devil's advocate.

Develop a script—commentators or politicians might call it "talking points"—that can help you feel self-assured when the red light comes on. That, along with several deep breaths and reminding yourself that you know what you're talking about, should help calm you for an effective interview.

꙳

In 2000 my writing partner, Jeff Barker, was asked to appear on the *PBS NewsHour* to discuss the upcoming Arizona Republican presidential primary pitting John McCain, George W. Bush, Steve Forbes, and Pat Buchanan against one another. Jeff was then a reporter for the *Arizona Republic* newspaper and was familiar with the state's voting demographic and the issues in the campaign.

He had some television and radio experience, but broadcast was not his primary medium. So he prepared a little differently than he would for a newspaper story. He established a basic goal of reaching a stage where he felt relatively comfortable—there are always going to be some nerves—going on the show. "You know this stuff," he told himself. "Just take a deep breath and try to be yourself." He wore his favorite tie for good luck.

To feel confident, Jeff typed out a short list of facts and committed the important ones to memory: What was the voter turnout in comparable primaries? How much money had the candidates raised and spent? McCain, the home-state senator, was expected to win easily—and did—although the state's GOP governor, Jane Hull, had endorsed George W. Bush.

The challenging part of such interviews is that you can't always anticipate the interviewer's questions. Some news producers will offer specific or general guidance in advance on where the questions may be headed. But some leave it open-ended.

The McCain-Hull rift was clearly an interesting story line— a GOP governor not endorsing a GOP presidential candidate from her state—and Jeff prepared as if he would be asked about it (he was, although indirectly). He also prepared to provide a prediction on the outcome of the primary. That's a standard question whether you're discussing an election or a football game, and it was indeed posed by the interviewer, Gwen Ifill.

In addition to listing pertinent facts about the race, Jeff's "script" also contained some buzzwords. While you can't anticipate an interviewer's questions, you can develop some ready-made answers and look for openings to use them.

Beneath his list of facts, Jeff wrote two words: "Cowboy Hat."

He had previously developed a theory about Arizona politics—that the state considered itself as independent as an iconic cowboy and embraced maverick politicians. He was ready with an answer if asked to characterize the state's voting mood. His buzzwords—which he repeated a few times to himself before the interview—were intended to prompt his response.

When the interview began, he knew where he was headed midway through Gwen Ifill's first question.

> **Gwen Ifill:** Jeff Barker of the *Arizona Republic*, Arizona is home to both conservatives like Barry Goldwater and a liberal icon like Morris Udall. Who are the Arizona voters here?
>
> **Jeff Barker:** Well, Arizona is really quite a mix. I think that the social conservatives aren't quite as well organized here. I think the character of Arizona really is . . . can be symbolized by the cowboy hat. You know, candidates in Arizona always wear cowboy hats. Pat Buchanan wore a black hat when he ran here in '96. And I think it sort of symbolizes the Old West, the independence. And I guess you can see that's why John McCain is a pretty good fit in Arizona, because his whole presidential campaign is set up around being a maverick. That's his image. He's always been a guy who would symbolically wear a cowboy hat in Arizona.

While Jeff couldn't anticipate the direction of his interview with certainty, he could make an educated guess and script accordingly. That preparation helped him achieve his goal of remaining composed—of being himself—and served as a resource so he could respond confidently and effectively.

Keep in Mind:

- Research if you feel you need more information than your knowledge base.
- List pertinent facts in a script and be in basic command of them before the interview.

- Try to anticipate the interviewer's questions in your script.
- Remember you aren't totally captive to the questions. You can develop your own points and look for opportune moments to make them.
- Take slow, deep breaths if you are nervous. Remember that you probably know more about the topic than the person asking the questions. That's why you were selected for the interview.

CHAPTER 9

✳

Family

Asking a Potential Spouse for a Prenuptial Agreement

Few documents are as potentially sensitive as a legal and binding prenuptial agreement, which usually sets the ground rules for property division and postmarital payments in the event of a divorce. It is not associated with romance nor is it a popular conversation topic. Many individuals stress over how their potential spouse will react to a request for a prenuptial, worried that it may be viewed as an expectation of divorce or a demonstration of mistrust that could undermine the relationship.

Although advisers may strongly suggest it, a "prenup" is not for everyone. Those pursuing one will face the question of how to raise such a difficult subject without taking the bloom off the marital rose. It is up to legal and financial advisers to suggest approaches and to deal with the legal and financial issues. But it falls to the individual to find the right words with which to proceed.

As with any challenging conversation, managing the discussion requires precise timing and word choice, as well as acute sensitivity to the other party's feelings. The decision to move forward with a prenup is a very personal one requiring introspection. The wisdom of whether or not to insist on an agreement is beyond the scope of this chapter. It involves a very personal decision.

Scripting can help prepare for the conversation to introduce the topic comfortably and speak to a fiancé or fiancée with confidence. It can help avoid miscommunications and shape the expression of strong reasons for the request. When preparing the message, individuals should keep in mind their partner's feelings and be respectful of them.

The location of the discussion should be well thought out. The fiancé or fiancée should be informed of the need to discuss something important at a place free from any possible interruptions. Family gatherings, dinner parties, or other communal events are not suitable environments to bring up signing a prenuptial agreement.

It's best to avoid arriving at the initial meeting with a draft of the document because that conveys closed-mindedness. A person who feels the agreement is a fait accompli may well become defensive. This result would inhibit discussion and could threaten the engagement. Instead, approach the first conversation as a give-and-take on the subject in which both sides have an equal voice.

It can be helpful to begin the discussion by introducing the subject as part of a larger plan. The goals and role of a prenuptial agreement can be useful in relation to other legal planning and choices that a couple will have to work through. If one has accumulated, created, or inherited wealth, discussing the roots of it—and the intended use of the assets—openly can help diminish any mistrust that may arise as a result of the request.

Throughout the conversation, it's wise to candidly restate the desire to marry. No one wants to hear about the end of the marriage before it has begun.

At the end of the initial delivery, the fiancé or fiancée should be given time to process the information, consider the proposal, and prepare a response of his or her own. And encouraging the person to have his or her own counsel should be communicated before the conversation ends. In the final analysis, reaching an agreement may only be achieved, if at all, after extensive discussions.

✳

After two and a half years of dating, Tommy proposed to Ashley outside the coffee shop where they had first met. The two were deeply in love and excited to spend the rest of their lives together. When Ashley's parents heard the news, however, they informed their daughter that, unless Tommy signed a prenuptial agreement, she would be cut out of their will. Ashley came from a very wealthy family and her parents wanted to make sure that the future earnings from her share of the family's wealth would be protected.

Ashley was initially nervous that Tommy might perceive the request as her having doubts and worried he might even break off the engagement. However, having watched a friend go through a messy divorce, she decided that having a prenuptial agreement was a precaution she would pursue. She had seen her friend and the friend's husband—once loving and supportive of each other—transformed during the divorce. They were each now bitter and ruthless when it came to the other. Knowing the statistical likelihood of divorce, Ashley wanted to be sure that if a divorce were to occur, decisions would be made based on love rather than volatile emotions. She also felt that her share of her family's wealth warranted protection. Nevertheless, Ashley was still nervous about initiating the conversation.

Therefore, after talking to her personal lawyer, she used the scripting process to ensure that she would confidently deliver the right message. Ashley wrote a draft of her script and then asked her older sister and the sister's husband, who had signed a prenuptial agreement two years earlier, to act as her devil's advocates and give her feedback.

Once she felt ready, Ashley e-mailed Tommy and asked if they could switch their dinner date that evening from their favorite restaurant to her apartment. That way, Tommy could react without being inhibited by the setting. At their dinner, Ashley communicated the following message.

Tommy,

Ever since our picnic in Central Park last year, I knew I wanted to marry you. Words cannot express how much I love you and what you have grown to mean to me. And I am so excited about our wedding and life together.

And those feelings should not be obscured by what I want to discuss this evening—the possibility of us signing a prenuptial agreement. This is neither a sign of mistrust nor an expectation of our marriage failing, but is a reasonable way of giving my family a sense of security that the wealth they have built will stay in the family. My folks feel strongly about this and my sister and her husband have found it has not affected their relationship.

In addition, planning this is also an effective way to review our future goals and financial objectives, as well as to discuss our expectations of each other once we are married.

Do you have any questions? [Give Tommy time to respond.]

Please take all the time you need to reflect on what I said. And certainly talk to your lawyer as we will each need our own lawyer to help us with this. And don't forget, my love for you is no way impacted by wanting a prenuptial agreement. I want to marry you now as much as ever.

After hearing her out, Tommy said little. Rather than arguing or asking questions, he switched to other subjects. When Ashley tried to engage him on the subject the next day, he said he needed some time to think about it. Subsequently, Ashley received an e-mail from Tommy in which he stated that—while he truly believed Ashley and could understand her parents' perspective—he was not willing to go into a marriage with an agreement that focused on filling a need should it end. He also stated: "Maybe it's best that we postpone the wedding. I hope you understand my feelings."

Several weeks and discussions later, Ashley and Tommy decided to go forward with the wedding without a prenuptial agreement. Although their relationship suffered some temporary strain from the discussion, their love remained strong. And when the wedding did occur, Ashley's parents were in attendance. Her father told her he would "wait and see" how things went between Ashley and Tommy before taking any action regarding Ashley's inheritance. So although the scripting process did not achieve getting the prenuptial agreement done, it did allow for an exchange of views without destroying the relationship. Scripts aren't panaceas, but in some cases they still can stem the tide of destructive emotions.

Keep in Mind:

- Conduct the conversation in a private setting to permit a free flow of ideas or at least not inhibit emotions.
- Do not present a document at the first meeting. The conversation should be approached as a give-and-take between equals.
- Reaffirm your love and desire to marry as a part of the conversation—it's not about a lack of faith in the relationship, but rather a pragmatic planning step supported by experience.
- Give your partner time to digest and get his or her own counsel.
- You may not succeed and will then have to decide whether or not having an agreement is worth the risk of losing the marriage.

Talking to Your Kids about Sex

In the best cases, parents and children enjoy an open flow of discussion on a wide array of topics. While some topics may easily come up in casual conversation, there are a few subjects—especially those relating to sex—that are too complicated or weighty to emerge in the daily back-and-forth. Often, a vague response can satisfy a young child's prying questions, but later comes the need for detail and clarity, and possibly even a discussion about pregnancy and sexually transmitted diseases. In this section we focus on that first conversation in the preteen or early teen years.

Discussing sex should be viewed as an ongoing conversation rather than a onetime lecture in which the parent is talking to—but not actually with—the child. Parents and teenagers may find the topic easier to discuss while engaged in other activities, such as cooking, eating, or driving. Although it can be tempting for parents to immediately make judgmental statements about sex-related issues, this should not be communicated in the first conversation. The goal of this message is to open the lines for future communications. This will not happen if the child fears being judged or senses closed-mindedness from the parent. There are moments in day-to-day life in which sex discussions may occur naturally. For example, if a song with sexually graphic lyrics comes on the radio, a parent could ask, "Do you know what [these specific lyrics] mean? I'm surprised this singer would say this about herself." Asking questions like this allows parents to transition into conversations about sex that don't feel forced.

The scripting process will assist the parent in sharing the best message by laying out thoughts, making revisions, and practicing in advance. And it will help build the parents' comfort level with what will be said on the subject.

It's important not to be discouraged if the child attempts to shut down the conversation. A parent can prepare for this reaction by having responses at hand to calm the teenager down and resume an open dialogue. To a dismissive "hmm" or rolling of the eyes, a parent could say, "I'm not asking you to share anything private, just to listen with an open mind and know I'm here to answer any future questions."

Kids should be given an opportunity to share what they have been told by others. This step can provide parents with a distinct platform for the talk and a chance to clear up any inaccurate information. In order to create a comfortable setting, parents should avoid disputing their child's opinions, making demands, or assuming the child craves guidance. Some statements are immediate conversation stoppers. These include "You're too young to understand," "I don't care what your friends are doing, these are my rules," and "Are you asking me that because you are planning to do it?"

A game plan in a two-parent home might be for one parent to write the initial draft of the script and the other to be the devil's advocate. Grandparents, friends, or other family members familiar with this situation can act as devil's advocates for single parents. Parents can then smoothly transition into sharing with their daughters or sons what they want them to know, while demonstrating an understanding of what their kids are experiencing and the environment they live in.

☀

Last fall, my friend Kelly's daughter, Megan, was starting the fifth grade. Kelly was anxious about having "the sex talk" with Megan and was unsure if it was even the right time. Kelly's nerves were on edge because she did not know, especially with modern media's aggressive portrayal of sex, what information her daughter already had about sex. It was important for Kelly not only to educate her daughter, but to create an environment where Megan felt comfortable being honest.

After Kelly received an e-mail from Megan's school informing her that a sex education speaker would be visiting Megan's class that semester, Kelly decided the time had come to start conversations about sex. She remembered her own confusion and fear as a young girl when she first heard about sex from a stranger rather than her parents.

Kelly was familiar with my scripting process and decided to

draft what she wanted to say and then have her husband, Mark, read it over. Kelly's first draft was filled with long explanations about the dangers of sex, including stories involving sexually transmitted diseases, pregnancy, and the psychological effects of having sex too young. This flood of information would likely have not only terrified Megan, but confused her; and it missed the purpose. This first conversation needed to aim to open the door for future talks. Mark reorganized and simplified Kelly's script. Using Mark's edits, she changed her script into a straightforward message intended to make Megan comfortable discussing sex-related topics with her mother.

Megan,

　　I received an e-mail from your teacher that a woman will be coming to your class soon to discuss sex. I know this can be an uncomfortable subject to talk about. I myself feel awkward talking about a few of the topics sometimes, but it's still important that we do so to help you get good information and avoid misunderstandings. I wish that I could have talked with my mom about sex—then maybe I wouldn't have been so confused about it as long as I was. And I know that in the world you are growing up in, the information and ideas you get from TV, the Internet, and friends is much more than I ever had and can make things even more confusing.

　　Do you have any questions or are you confused about anything you've heard from friends or television? [Listen to her talk and then answer those questions without bias. If you are unsure how to answer, tell her you will do some checking on that point and will follow up within the next few days.]

　　I know you're only ten and hopefully there are topics we will not need to discuss until later on, but I want you to know now my feelings on certain things. It is my opinion as your mom that you should not engage in a physical relationship until you are both in a committed relationship and have emotionally matured. Does this make sense to you? [Allow her to respond.] When the time comes that you disagree, don't understand, or think my thoughts don't make sense, I want you to let me know and feel free to discuss it with me. I'm willing to keep an open mind if you are. Does this sound like a good idea to you? [Allow her to respond.]

Please know that you can approach me free of judgment with any questions or concerns you have about sex.

Do you have any other questions or concerns for me? I hope this will be the first of many conversations to come. And please remember that I am trying to help you understand some very sensitive ideas and not just force my views on you. I love you.

Although Megan seemed tense at the beginning of the conversation, by the end she was comfortably talking to her mother about her perceptions and concerns. Kelly was relieved that her daughter now knew she was available to discuss these issues and was not afraid to do so. And as time passed, their conversations about sex continued.

Keep in Mind:

- Have the conversation in a safe, comfortable environment without distractions.
- Asking children to share what they have been previously told on the subject can provide parents with a distinct starting point and a chance to clear up any inaccurate information.
- Parents should demonstrate an understanding of what their kids are experiencing and the environment in which they

live without presuming they are identical to their children. Their experiences are their own; they are maturing in a different generation.

- Have responses prepared for different reactions and possible questions.
- Leave the conversation with the child feeling that the discussion will be ongoing—and that he or she shouldn't hesitate to come with additional questions or concerns that may arise.

Talking to Your Kids about a National Tragedy

National tragedies—such as 9/11, the December 2012 Connecticut school shootings, or other horrific events—affect us all. These are emotional times for the country and present an array of complicated feelings for citizens. There is inevitably sadness, anger at the perpetrators, and, eventually, a transition back to our routines.

The immediate aftermath can be a vexing time for the parents of young children. With the media's ceaseless coverage—as well as anticipated chatter at school—parents can't help but ask themselves questions about their children. What have they heard? How much, if anything, should I tell them?

The goal here, of course, is to do what's best for the child. There may be a temptation for parents or other adults to say too much. A guideline is to let the children themselves provide the cues. In their own way, kids will often let you know what they're ready to hear.

Consider a child who believes in Santa Claus. At some point, most children will begin to ask questions about whether Santa Claus exists. Their curiosity—and reaction to adults' responses to their questions—provides signals about the children's mind-set and how far they are able to proceed.

After mass murders or other tragedies, parents should resist providing too much information, too soon. KJ Dell'Antonia, who authors a family blog for the *New York Times*, wrote after the Connecticut school tragedy:

"As a parent, you're left with the question not just of how to talk to your child about tragedy, but of whether you're talking to your child for your child—or for yourself. There's the question of what to say, but also when, and if, you should say it."

The days following such events are times to monitor children even more closely than normal. Parents or other adults should limit kids' exposure to media covering the events, particularly if there is no grown-up available to discuss what is unfolding.

Kids are often adept at picking up on their parents' moods and may sense that something is amiss. Children may ask their parents whether something is wrong. That's the time to provide reassurance.

Most kids know there is evil in the world. What they need to hear is that most people are not evil, and that their own environments—their schools and homes—are safe and that grown-ups are looking after them.

In December 2012, the National Association of School Psychologists provided tips on its website for helping children cope following the shootings in Newtown, Connecticut.

- Provide a developmentally appropriate, clear, and straight-forward explanation of the event.
- Return to normalcy and routine to the best extent possible while maintaining flexibility.

- Let children know it's okay to feel upset or angry.
- Be a good listener and observer.
- Provide various ways for children to express emotion, either through journaling, writing letters, talking, making a collage, or music.
- Focus on resiliency as well as the compassion of others.

Such tips are useful in a broad sense. But since every child is different, every conversation children have with their parents or other caretakers will be different, too.

That's where scripting can help. Writing out talking points and contingencies can help ensure you have the right words at the right time for your child.

❋

Zachary, a second-grader, was at his Virginia school when the news broke that a gunman had killed twenty children and six adults at Sandy Hook Elementary School in Newtown, Connecticut.

Zachary's school—like many around the country—tightened security procedures. But the school made the decision not to make any announcements or have any meetings about the Connecticut shootings. It left the decision on informing kids (or not informing them) to parents, although it said counselors and school psychologists would be available, if needed.

When Zachary got off the school bus that afternoon, his mother watched him closely. He skipped and danced around and chatted with a friend as he walked home. Nothing appeared different, and it seemed likely to his mother that he had not heard anything about the tragedy.

A day passed with no mention in Zachary's family of the shooting. But two nights after the shooting, Zachary noticed his mother sitting on the couch crying. She had been watching television coverage of the planned funerals and had been overcome with grief.

Zachary asked his mother what was wrong. She smiled through her tears and said something sad had occurred—she made it immediately clear nothing had happened to their own family. She then called her husband downstairs so they could talk together to their son.

Fortunately, Zachary's mother was a born scripter. She had anticipated this conversation might occur and had jotted down some notes and rehearsed some dialogue, albeit only in her head.

> Zachary, somebody harmed some teachers and kids at a school in the state of Connecticut.
>
> We want you to know you are okay. Your school does a lot to keep kids safe. Mommy and Daddy would not send you anyplace we thought was unsafe.
>
> You might hear about this from friends or on television. If you do, we'd like you to talk over what you hear with us to make sure it's true. We want you to get the best information.
>
> It's always sad when people get hurt. That's why Mommy was crying. But we're fine. We'll just give each other extra hugs.
>
> Do you have any questions?

Zachary did have a question. It was perhaps the toughest question of all: "Why would somebody hurt children?"

His parents had prepared the best answer they knew:

> We don't know; something was wrong with him. The grown-ups that you know—our close friends and family— love you and would never do something bad to a child.

Keep in Mind:

- Be truthful, but resist the temptation to say too much too soon.
- Listen for cues from your children as to what they are developmentally ready to hear and when they are ready to hear it.
- Reassure children that adults in their schools and homes are taking measures to keep them safe.
- Explain that's it's okay for parents to be sad, and that their grief is natural and not something to worry about.

Nudging an Adult Child Out of the House

Parenthood blesses many with the joys and challenges of watching children grow. Special moments—the first steps, riding a bicycle for the first time, the first day of school, holiday meals together, meeting a prom date—occur at home and become inseparable from the location itself. Even as children grow into adulthood, some may continue to live in their parents' house, particularly in a struggling economy. Most parents who can afford it jump at the opportunity to offer such support for their now-grown children. But there comes a time when the parents logically conclude that it will be in everyone's best interest that the children move out. Getting a young adult to find a place of his or her own, however, can be difficult to execute, particularly if expectations have not been managed.

The important thing to remember is that moving out can be a positive step. A move may enhance your son's or daughter's independence while reducing the parents' economic and psychological pressures. So asking the grown child to move out should not be a rash decision, but should be built upon a clear understanding that it is the right time. Perhaps some old Ann Landers advice will help raise the parents' confidence: "In the final analysis it is not what you do for your children, but what you have taught them to do for themselves that will make them successful human beings." Fears of upsetting the child have to be set aside and can be mitigated by the clearly expressed hope of leading them to a more independent life.

The discussion might begin with an expression of how blessed the parents feel to have shared the house to this point. That may be followed by an honest statement about why the young adult needs to find a place of his or her own. The reasons should be clearly stated—that the goal is for the child to achieve independence while the parents reclaim their home. If there is to be a transition period (one to two months, for example), the conditions should be communicated: paying rent or doing one's own laundry may come into play here. A move-out gift may also be suggested—perhaps a relocation payment if the parents have the means. A firm decision does not have to preclude willingness to help with the move—assisting with apartment hunting and helping sort out options.

※

One morning, while brewing a cup of coffee, Nancy, an intern in my office, told me a story from her past weekend. Nancy had spent her Sunday afternoon helping her friend Samantha frame and hang pictures in her new apartment. Nancy found their day together to be especially enjoyable because Samantha was finally becoming independent from her family and, although she was at first resentful of her parents' move-out demands, was now easing into her new living condition.

After college, Samantha took a marketing job at low pay within three months of graduation. Recognizing that her income would not support her even at a minimal level, she accepted her parents' invitation to move back home and use the opportunity to save money. She was not always happy about parental restrictions on her comings and goings. And her parents would occasionally lament the loss of space they had gained while she was away at school. But, overall, the living arrangement seemed to suffice for over a year.

During that period, Samantha received several raises and began to earn a "living wage." At one point, her parents talked to her about charging a nominal rent, but they did not follow through. Eventually her parents felt that the time had come to reclaim their privacy and that Samantha should be focusing not only on her professional development but on building her personal independence. The topic was initially broached during a family meal in the beginning of November that was also attended by Samantha's two older brothers—one married and the other living two states away. Then, after Thanksgiving dinner, her parents informed Samantha that by the first of the new year they wanted her moved out.

Prior to the discussion, her mother had scratched out some thoughts on a pad on what she wanted to say to Samantha. Her mother shared those notes with her dad. After he made revisions, she felt comfortable in communicating the following post–Thanksgiving dinner message to her daughter.

Your father and I were really pleased when you told us how well your job is going and that your good work has been recognized with nice raises. We hope that you living here over the past year or so has helped you get on your feet financially and allowed you to focus on your job rather than worry about how you were going to support yourself. [Ask: "What do you think about the time you have spent here since college?]

[Assuming the answer recognizes the benefits of having lived at home.] Your dad and I now feel that this is the perfect time for you to begin making plans to move out and into your own space. We suggest that you find an apartment and plan to move out after the holidays—the first of the year should work well for all of us.

I am happy to help you go apartment hunting. We have also decided that as a contribution to your launching yourself on the road to an independent life, we would like to help you buy a couch and a bed for your new apartment as well as give you a gift of paying for the first month's rent.

We'll miss seeing you on a regular basis, but just as your dad and I need some more time together, we know that you will benefit from building a life of your own away from this home. Do you have any questions? [Circle back and reiterate that Samantha is expected to be in her new apartment by the first of the new year.]

Initially, Samantha was not happy with the request. She felt somewhat betrayed by her parents as she ate her first meal in the new apartment on January 5. Nevertheless, after getting advice from her older brothers and using Nancy as a support system, Samantha retreated from her anger and recognized that she was fortunate to have lived the last fifteen months at home while her income grew sufficiently to afford her own place. Her parents' gesture of furniture and a month's rent was a warm gift that allowed her to ease into independence.

Keep in Mind:

- Give suggestions that will help transition your child into his or her own place.
- Begin the dialogue in an appreciative tone. Tell your child how much you love him or her and how proud you are of him or her.
- Be direct about why your child needs to move out—covering both personal and monetary reasons.
- Allow your child to push back and respond so his or her opinions are also expressed.
- Communicate that if your child intends to stay for any additional agreed-upon period, he or she must pay rent and respect your rules.

Managing a Budget between Spouses

Sound marital relationships are filled with more highs than lows. But regardless of a relationship's strength, differences of opinion are likely to occur over how the two spend their money. Personality, upbringing, values, and expectations all can affect approaches to spending. The hope is always that a couple will collaborate in creating and enforcing budgets. Yet few marriages are free from one spouse seeking to convince another that a particular purchase is improvident.

Nobody likes to feel their spending is being limited inappropriately. When views on potential expenditures clash, emotional confrontations are likely to ensue. The partner being restrained may feel threatened or insulted and go into a reactive mode. If a couple continuously engages in such confrontations, there may be a divorce in their future—it has been reported that 32.9 percent of failed marriages are caused by financial problems. When addressing a proposed expenditure, it may be best to ask a few questions and listen rather than stating a hasty "no way." This will give time to put the scripting process into play and also provide a cooling-off period.

The scripting process provides a medium for a thoughtful, sensitive analysis that can lead to a constructive solution. When putting thoughts together, one party should not simply dismiss the other's idea or criticize his or her impulsive intent. Instead, the person should express a desire to work together as a team to find a mutually acceptable solution. It works better to show that the expenditure has been given consideration and suggest alternative ways to accomplish the original goal with a reduced spending plan.

✵

Charlie has been married to Ann for thirty-five years. There is no doubt in the minds of those who know them that their love and affection for each other are genuine. Since the day they met thirty-seven years ago, the two have supported each other through personal and professional challenges and shared a multitude of happy memories. Although their lives are not stress free—they disagree on politics and certain philosophical issues—Charlie and Ann share life experiences in ways many others wish they could.

But even Charlie and Ann are not immune from differences of opinion over spending. One evening, they joined me and my wife for dinner and shared a story with us. They can joke about it now. But when Ann first approached Charlie to excitedly tell him about a project she wanted to undertake, he did not consider it a laughing matter. Ann wanted to build a unique playhouse on their property for their increasing number—seven at the time—of grandchildren. She projected that the project would be easily completed since it would only require a toilet and sink—but no other significant utilities. She intended to design the house herself and work with moonlight laborers to keep expenses down.

Knowing his wife and her perfectionist nature, Charlie knew that although she may have set a $5,000 budget, the final cost of the project could be at least 50 percent greater. Charlie was in a transitional stage of his career and was uncertain about his income's stability over the next year. He was concerned about having enough cash to support the venture. The challenge for Charlie then became what to say to his wife and how to say it. The objective of building the playhouse was so firmly set in her mind that merely denying the funds would either be ignored or trigger a spousal battle.

Charlie first scribbled some thoughts, revised them, and weighed Ann's feelings as well as his own concerns. He then considered approaching Ann with his carefully scripted message. But Charlie decided that addressing the subject face-to-face might cause Ann to react negatively before he finished speaking. That could set the couple off into counterreactions because the topic was emotionally charged. Instead, Charlie sat down at a computer and typed the message to her. It was common for him to e-mail Ann—particularly when he was at work.

In his e-mail, Charlie made the choice not to simply tell Ann, "You can't build the playhouse." Instead, he raised questions about its feasibility and its impact on their budget in light of his income limitations. He was sharing his uneasiness as a partner rather than a financial dictator, and he meant every word he wrote to her.

Love,

I support the playhouse idea and look forward to seeing
some pictures. There are, however, two considerations that
I do not want to lose sight of: 1) My income this year is
dropping 60% and therefore the expenditure might be better
made next year—this year the kitchen renovation has put us
close to our budget limit; and 2) I do want to check the
restrictive covenants of the homeowners' association to make
sure we do not violate the "no new structures" limitation.

I assume that the structure can be built without the need
for electrical power and that it will not need a foundation, but
let me know if I am wrong. Those factors could be important
in analyzing the applicability of the homeowners' covenants.

I love you and admire your unbelievable creativity. I want
to work with you on a plan that works both financially and
legally. Thanks for making my life beautiful.

After reading his e-mail, Ann smiled. She was pleased that
Charlie had appreciated and taken a real interest in building a
playhouse. In return, she took time to reflect on the two points
Charlie had made and do further research on the idea.

Ann looked into a few different models and discovered that
designing her own playhouse would be significantly more expensive than she had originally speculated. She also recalled that
the homeowners' association had a history of denying any construction, like her planned playhouse, that could be seen from
the road. In addition, Ann had not taken into account the work
that had gone into their kitchen's recent makeover. Although she
was satisfied with the end result, the process had been over-
whelming at times and she was not inclined to throw herself into
another large project so soon. Instead, Ann and Charlie bought
a two-seated swing to hang from a large oak tree in the backyard

that their grandchildren enjoyed, even in the absence of a play-house.

Keep in Mind:

- Don't immediately offer a negative reply. Ask questions and allow time for a cooling-off period.
- Instead of dismissing the proposal out of hand, assess its merits while asking questions that show an appreciation for the idea but also the need for cost constraint.
- Note any impractical aspects of the project.
- Remember that suggestions of alternative, but less expensive, approaches can lead to a satisfactory compromise.
- Reaffirm that you admire your partner's accomplishments and intentions.

Telling Your Kids You Are Getting Divorced

Going through a divorce, however amicable, can fill a couple's life with stress and challenges. This is especially true when children are involved.

Divorcing parents may feel a wide range of emotions. These should be expressed to professionals, friends, and family members rather than vented to children. Research has revealed that divorce, managed poorly, can leave a lasting impression on children and cause them to carry scars into their future relationships. It is best to keep this in mind while you handle the delicate situation of informing your children.

Communicating to children a separation or divorce decision

will never be easy, even when you seek out and follow expert advice. Nevertheless, if parents plan what they will say prior to the meeting, they may be able to lessen the adverse impact by reducing potential misunderstandings and keeping themselves from making statements they may later regret. Scripting answers to possible questions and preparing restrained responses to any signs of each other's anger or hurt could reduce the emotional damage to children when they first hear the upsetting news.

When approaching this conversation, parents should consider several cautionary paths. Do not break the news of the divorce if one (or both) of the spouses is so distraught that he or she cannot contain volatile feelings. If possible, wait for both parties' outward emotions to cool before approaching the subject. Regardless of any anger either partner feels, or the validity of these feelings, each must refrain from blaming the other parent or venting about his or her faults. Because of the strong bond that children generally share with both parents, this type of blame or venting will only confuse children and leave them unsure of how to process it.

And leave time for the children to ask questions. It is likely that children will ask why the divorce is occurring. Initially, parents can prepare for this by crafting a response using "we" in their explanation to emphasize the decision is mutual. Planning a message that neither places blame nor dwells on many details may help provide children with a reasonable explanation without feeling they are being put in the middle.

If possible, parents should give the news together so the children only hear one shared story. Parents might try to establish what their children already know about divorce and the state of their marriage so they can construct the communication in a manner the children will understand. Deliver the message clearly that, in the long run, this is the best decision for the family. Keep the conversation simple to avoid confusion, and explain the plan of action. This may provide a sense of stability despite the drastic life alteration. Offering clarity as to when the official separation will take place, who is moving out, when the children will see that parent, where they will live, and any other details of their current life that may be affected by the decision may alleviate concerns, expressed or not, of the children.

In addition, it's critical to emphasize to children that the divorce is not their fault and although the parents may no longer be in love, it has no effect on the love they feel toward their children. Inform them that the divorce is not the result of their actions, such as failing to complete chores, and therefore, a change in the children's behavior will not mend the marriage.

※

Sharron and Kyle, former neighbors of mine, had been married for fourteen years and blessed with two children, Megan and Gus, ages twelve and eight. Although for the first ten years of their marriage they were apparently happy, the last four years had been a struggle. After Kyle got laid off from work, they found themselves continuously arguing over financial matters. In addition, each was growing increasingly frustrated with the habits of the other—Sharron became less interested in spending time with Kyle, and Kyle frequently chose to attend functions with friends rather than spend time with his family.

After four months of counseling, the two finally came to the conclusion that the flame of their love had burned out. Nevertheless, they decided to try to stay together "for the children."

This decision, however, only compounded tensions—hardly a day passed without an argument breaking out, sometimes even in front of the children. It became clear they would not be able to make the marriage work in a manner that would provide their children with a loving and nurturing environment and themselves with personal happiness.

After talking with a counselor and with good friends who had experienced a similar communication challenge after a decision to divorce, Sharron and Kyle sat down one afternoon while the children were at school to discuss what they would say. They then wrote a draft of what they planned to tell Megan and Gus. Although they struggled over the text, both agreed upon a script that would both inform their children of the decision as well as seek to reassure them that there was a stable plan for the children's future and that they were still greatly loved.

On Saturday afternoon, after Megan came home from Girl Scouts and Gus from his junior league soccer game, they all sat down in the living room together. Sharron and Kyle took turns delivering the following message.

> Kids,
> We have something important to tell you that will not be easy to say. Although Mom and Dad used to love each other, for the past year or so we have not been happy together. As you may have noticed, we have been arguing a lot and not working as a team. We talked to a counselor and have tried to make it work, but now we have decided that it is in our family's best interest that we get a divorce. Do you know what this means? [Give them time to respond.]
> Our divorce is not anyone's fault. Please do not blame yourselves or think there is something you can do differ-

ently to change our decision. In life, relationships, even between a married couple, sometimes stop working and a change needs to be made to avoid more unhappiness. We still love you two just the same. Nothing will ever change that.

In two weeks Dad will be moving into an apartment several miles from here. We have decided that it is best that you two will still live here and see Dad every weekend and for dinner at least twice a week. Everything else will remain the same. [Do you guys have any questions?]

We're so sorry to have to put you through this, but we ultimately believe it is in everyone's best interest. Please come talk to us about any questions, concerns, or thoughts about this whenever you want. We love both of you so much.

Although Megan and Gus were at first startled and Megan began to cry, after their parents reassured them that they would not be giving up a parent and that the divorce would not dislocate them from their home or schools, they began to calm down. And as time passed, they felt comfortable enough to approach their parents to talk further about the divorce. Sharron and Kyle's honesty about the situation and the children's future as well as their mutual explanation made a hitherto unthinkable situation bearable.

Keep in Mind:

- When delivering the message, parents should be clear that this is the final decision and that there is a plan about how exactly the children's life will be altered and affected.
- Remind the children that the divorce is not their fault and that they are still loved by both parents.

- Avoid making accusations or blaming the other parent.
- If possible, parents should deliver the message together and during a time when the children will be free to ask questions or express concerns without rushing off to some activity or appointment.

Settling Family Inheritance Squabbles

Few sorts of disagreements test a family more than an inheritance dispute. It's not just the value of the inheritance itself that can turn families against themselves. There is often emotional weight attached to the object of the dispute.

It may be a piece of land that holds fond memories or a family heirloom with a complicated history. Often the skirmish over the property becomes complicated by old family rivalries or jealousies. The goal here is not only to settle the issue fairly, but to mitigate hurt feelings.

Scripting can set the stage for an exchange that minimizes squabbling while helping you get what you believe you deserve. The first step is to clearly stake out your claim through a draft script and test the impact of it on someone willing to be a tough devil's advocate. After getting input and adjusting the message, practicing your delivery will help you stay on point and keep the right tone, no matter the other party's reaction.

Recognizing that your relative's claim has some merit—and being a good listener—may lower the emotional flame and make it possible to maintain a relationship when the exchange is over.

If you are confident in your position, how you "close" will

be the ultimate test of the impact of your claim. And it might help avoid what could become a divided family and costly litigation.

☀

For years, Rachel's father and stepmother had lived in a large colonial home in Rhode Island. Rachel was in her forties and was a public relations executive in Washington, DC. She had children of her own.

The Rhode Island house had become a museum of sorts, filled with antique desks, tables, and artwork. Rachel had grown up surrounded by much of the old furniture before her parents' divorce and was familiar with it.

On a particular visit, her father asked if she liked a particular antique coffee table. He had grown fond of the table and said that he wanted her to have it after he died.

But here was the complication: before the table had arrived at Rachel's father's house years before, and become adopted by him, it had been part of her stepmother's family.

When her father died after a long illness, her stepmother decided it was time to move into assisted living. She then began the task of parceling out the furniture she could not take with her. She assigned the table to Rachel, who rented a moving van and transported it to her home.

Some months later, Rachel got an e-mail from one of her stepbrothers. His message said politely that the coffee table had been associated with his family and his upbringing. He asked if he could have it shipped to his home in Colorado.

Rachel knew she faced a delicate encounter. Her stepbrother was too far away to meet with in person, and e-mail seemed too impersonal. So she prepared to speak to him on the phone and explain why she was not granting his request.

After talking with her husband—her devil's advocate—she
wrote out "talking points" in what amounted to a rough script of
what she needed to say to her stepbrother. Her script, which she
could consult as she spoke on the phone, was intended not to be
read verbatim, but merely to keep her focused. If the conversation went badly, she was prepared to end it and try again on another day.

> I need to express my sadness. It's a difficult time for both of
> us. I lost a parent and you are worried about how your
> mother will cope in assisted living. We need to keep our
> eyes on the big picture.
> [Possible questions: How do you feel about all of this? Is
> there anything special that your mother needs that we may
> not be aware of?]
> I also want to address the coffee table situation. I know
> the coffee table was part of your history. But it's part of my
> history, too, through my father and his wishes. Like the
> family itself, the table has a blended history.
> And both my dad and your mom wanted me to have it.
> It probably would have been best if we had discussed the
> table beforehand. But our folks made a decision and it is in
> our home now.
> ["So can we move forward on that basis?" If negative,
> repeat prior position.]

With the aid of the script, the conversation was short and
remained on point. Although he initially pushed back on Rachel's request, her stepbrother ceased staking his claim. The
coffee table remained in Rachel's home. The ending wasn't
perfect—she sometimes found herself wondering if there was a
solution that could have been more accommodating to her stepbrother. But the immediate matter had been put to rest without

enmity, and she felt as if her stepbrother better understood her attachment to the table.

Keep in Mind:

- You can't script emotions. But developing a script can keep you on topic in emotionally charged moments.
- Remember that inheritance disputes come at difficult times. Sharing feelings of grief can help defuse tense situations.
- Keep the matter in perspective by remembering "the big picture." Acknowledge your relative's point of view.
- As you close, unambiguously stake your claim.
- Be prepared to end the conversation and resume another day. Sometimes people need time to reflect before doing the right thing.

Taking the Car Keys Away from an Elderly Loved One

Driving a car has become one of life's necessities, but the privilege presumes that you can drive without endangering others. Elderly drivers may not satisfy that safety condition. Vivid examples of the perils of driving at an advanced age fill the airwaves. Particularly tragic is the story of George Weller, age eighty-nine, who in the summer of 2006 drove his car into a Santa Monica open-air farmers' market, killing ten and injuring over seventy. Weller, in his advanced age, panicked as he approached the market and confused the accelerator with the brake pedal. He collided at over sixty miles per hour with the market's customers and employees. Weller's vehicle went almost three hundred yards before crashing into a ditch. While Weller's terrible accident may be extreme in the numbers killed and injured, accidents harming others do occur with some frequency because of elderly drivers.

Drivers over eighty are more likely than others to become a fatality in traffic collisions. Old age is often accompanied by a decrease in motor skills, thought processing, and memory.

The risks are many—losing control at high speeds, making sudden stops and lane changes, pressing the wrong pedals, and steering erratically—and all create the potential for accidents. The issue then arises: how to persuade longtime drivers to hand over their keys.

Few want to give up driving and the accompanying sense of independence and mobility. Countless daily activities—visiting friends, eating at restaurants, shopping at the mall, going to the movies—require transportation. While public transportation is often an option, there is a convenience attached to driving yourself. While surrendering the keys might be a matter of basic logic and safety, the elderly driver may view it as a loss of dignity and the end of the self-sufficient life they once knew. Surrendering the right to drive is especially tough for seniors who may also be coping with the mounting loss of friends and loved ones.

The message can be difficult to deliver. But it's easier to hear it from someone the driver knows cares about him or her— rather than the courts or the state agency overseeing motor vehicle licensing or, worst of all, as the result of a terrible accident. Taking the keys away from a parent or elderly loved one may solidify the swap of family positions—the child transitions to caretaker, and the parent becomes the one being cared for.

Telling a respected adult that he or she has become inept at what was once a simple task may be another embarrassing reminder of one's progression into unrecoverable dependence.

A carefully thought-out and scripted message may lessen the tension and increase the likelihood of a positive result. You will want to convey that you understand what this sacrifice means—not just harp on the potential dangers of continued driving. Providing examples of the potential and actual dangers—after first showing compassion and sensitivity—may help you to make the case.

Chances are that the person may be aware of the change in his or her driving ability, but is afraid to publicly acknowledge it. Responses like "I need to go to the pharmacy every week" or "How else will I make it to my book club?" are not uncommon as last-ditch efforts to demonstrate a need for independent transportation. Suggesting alternatives may help. Options such as creating a carpool schedule or using a driving service may lessen the fear of giving up the car. If all else fails, you can raise the possibility of completing an unsafe-driver report with the state department of motor vehicles. That may be the inevitable close to the conversation.

❋

Teresa, a fellow faculty member when I taught at a law school in the 1980s, sat in her living room chair mulling over a dilemma involving her father. When she'd arrived home from the office that afternoon, Teresa had listened to a voice mail from her mother explaining that her father was "fine," but she wanted Teresa to know that that morning he'd nearly totaled his car in an accident. Her mother continued: "I'm really afraid that although this most recent accident did not hurt anyone, sooner or later his erratic driving is going to cause some real harm to himself and others."

Teresa knew that her eighty-four-year-old father had reached the point where he needed to stop driving, but she was unsure how to approach the topic with him. Her father, always wanting to be in control, was not one to relinquish his keys easily and depend on other means of transportation. He had been a powerful CEO and, although he had been retired for the last fourteen years, a sense of autonomy was still a major part of his makeup. Her mother would not be of much help because she had a history of not confronting her husband.

The day following her father's crash, Teresa went online and read various web pages relating to driving and age. The one she found to be the most helpful was at the site Caring.com (www .caring.com/older-drivers), which had numerous articles covering a range of situations centered on discussing driving with elders. After researching, reflecting, and talking with her mother, Teresa practiced and delivered the message to her father.

> Dad,
> You are a very independent person and I've always admired you for it. I know that driving means a lot to you. To this day I still remember stories you told me about your first car. I've been wondering, however: how has driving been for you lately? [Allow him to respond and talk about his driving.]
> I asked you this because some of my friends' parents have been in car accidents lately—one of which tragically resulted in a father's death. This, along with your recent accident and changes I've noticed with your driving, deeply worries me that an accident harming—possibly killing— you or someone else may occur. Research shows that older drivers are significantly more likely to seriously injure or

kill themselves and others. [If he begins to push back, provide him with solid examples of changes with his driving such as, "You have a harder time turning your head than you used to" or "You braked suddenly at stop signs three times the last time we drove."]

The family and I want you to hand over your car keys and promise to refrain from operating any vehicles in the future. I understand that this is not an easy thing to do. However, safety must come first. Giving up driving doesn't mean you'll be stuck in the house. The public transportation system has improved over the last decade and there are many affordable driving services. I'm also here to provide you and Mom with any rides to the best of my ability.

I could not have asked for better parents than you and Mom. You took such great care of me while I lived in this house and I worry that I will be unable to return the favor to the same extent if you continue to use the car. [If he still refuses to stop driving, be prepared to deliver the bottom line of intending to seek the state's assistance to officially remove him from his car.]

As she delivered the message, Teresa's father, Harry, stared directly at her and was silent for what felt like an eternity but, in reality, was only thirty seconds. Harry finally responded by saying, "What do you think we can get for the car?" He then reached in his pocket, pulled out his keys, and offered them to her. Not every situation is so quickly resolved, but following Teresa's example of carefully preparing and scripting a message will raise the likelihood of moving the elderly driver from behind the wheel to the passenger seat.

Keep in Mind:

- Approach the conversation compassionately and convey an understanding of what this sacrifice means.
- Provide examples of hazardous driving and reminders of potential dangers.
- Allow the driver to explain how he or she views his or her own driving and probe objections to discover why the driver needs the car. Explore alternatives to being behind the wheel.
- If the driver refuses to hand over the keys, be prepared as a last resort to deliver a firm statement of your intention to seek official means to end the continued driving.

CHAPTER 10

✳

Friends

Asking a Roommate to Move Out

Sharing the rent of a home or apartment—with a friend or a stranger—has emerged in challenging economic times as a popular way to manage higher living costs and reduced incomes. Having a roommate may do more than reduce the burden of the monthly obligation to a landlord; it may also offer companionship to fill lonely moments. At best, the relationship clicks and, except for a spat or two along the way, continues without major incidents. But substantial changes in one's personal life or unpleasant experiences due to a poor choice in a rent partner may necessitate asking the roommate to move on, assuming the legal right exists.

If it is not a close relationship and the roommate is fairly passive, the task may be relatively easy. On the other hand, if the relationship runs deep or the roommate is aggressive, the discussion may be more challenging. In either case, the scripting process may empower the deliverer of the message.

The main benefit of the script is to keep the conversation on point. This is potentially a delicate conversation because it is not just a business deal—there is often a friendship involved. The script can help navigate an appropriate middle ground between being assertive—delivering the point succinctly—and acknowledging and being respectful of the roommate's feelings. Striking such a balance is not always an easy task.

※

Veronica and Joyce had lived together for eighteen months in an apartment overlooking Rittenhouse Square in Philadelphia. They were able to live in such a nice location because they shared the rent. Since the lease was under Veronica's name and she had the larger room overlooking the square, she paid a larger share. Their relationship flourished. They not only shared the apartment, but went to movies and concerts together, visited museums, and frequently enjoyed each other's company at dinner. In addition, when one was faced with a personal or professional challenge, the other provided emotional support.

Veronica had lived with Joyce for nearly fourteen months when Dave came into Veronica's life. The relationship grew to the point that being with Dave filled most of Veronica's free time. While she cherished memories of time spent with Joyce, she now longed for the ability to use the apartment as she saw fit—most important having Dave spend increasing amounts of time there. In addition, her professional career was flourishing: she had been promoted and received a healthy pay increase. So Veronica decided it was time to end her apartment-sharing relationship.

This posed a challenge. She and Joyce had had no prior discussion of a dissolution of their arrangement, and Veronica felt somewhat responsible for Joyce's well-being. Consequently, it was uncomfortable for Veronica to ask Joyce—whom she now considered a friend—to find new accommodations and was uncertain how to structure such a conversation.

After attending a public seminar I had presented in Philadelphia and learning about the concept of scripting, Veronica decided to take a stab at it herself. She wanted to acknowledge her warm feelings for Joyce and her hope for a continued friendship. But she also needed to firmly state that they had reached the end of their time as roommates.

Veronica decided to express her positive feelings for Joyce prior to delivering the tough news in case Joyce shut down emotionally after hearing she would have to move out. The script she used is appropriate for situations when there are no legal obligations but there is a desire to attempt to preserve a personal relationship.

> Joyce,
>
> It's hard to believe that we've spent almost two years together in this apartment. And I want you to know how much I have appreciated sharing experiences with you and the support we have provided each other during that time. I truly hope that the friendship we have built will last us a lifetime. I don't know what your plans are for the future, but I have given some thought to mine and have decided that for the next year or so I need this apartment for myself so that David and I can have the space to allow our relationship to develop. [There may be pushback here like, "I can stay out of your way." Be ready to respond with something like, "I understand where you're coming from and appreciate your willingness to stay out of the way, but I truly want to have total control over my life at this point and not have a roommate. If I were ever to

have a roommate again you would be the first person I would turn to."]

I recognize that this may be hard for you to deal with, but I also want you to know that I'm happy to have you take the next thirty days to find a new place for yourself.

Why don't we go out together this weekend and go apartment hunting? I would ask that you move out by [name a date], so looking this weekend would make sense. [If you get more push-back be ready with: "This may be hard for you to understand now, but I know you will later. I have made my decision and I just want to help you, to the extent that you want me to, in order to make the move as easy as possible for you."]

Do you have any questions?

About a year and a half later I received an e-mail from Veronica recounting this story and telling me how her courage had begun to fail her in the days leading up to this conversation with Joyce. But knowing the script—and having planned for several contingencies—gave her strength and allowed her to stick to her decision and remain composed during the conversation. She also informed me that a little over a year after her roommate moved out, she and David got married and Joyce was a bridesmaid in their wedding.

Keep in Mind:

- Begin the conversation by informing your roommate how much you appreciate him or her and how highly you view your relationship.
- Remain composed and firm in your decision.
- Be prepared for push-back and see if you can employ some contingency planning to help deliver your message.

- Offer solutions and be understanding that it may take time to find new accommodations.

Breaking Up with a Girlfriend or Boyfriend

As the song says, "breaking up is hard to do." Can scripting make it a bit easier? Carefully crafting and practicing a message beforehand may well keep the conversation from running on emotional reactions and counterreactions, which can lead to misconstrued communications. Each relationship is unique and there is not one standard type of statement to make. But taking the time to generate a carefully crafted message can aid in ending a relationship peacefully. Breakups can summon deep feelings—loss, sadness, anger. Feelings do not follow scripts. But scripting and some rehearsing may send the message through the wall of those emotions, or at the very least allow to you to say exactly what you mean.

A main focus of the conversation is the definitiveness of the separation. The goal is not to "take some time apart," or engage in an off-and-on-again romance that many couples fall into, but to end the relationship cleanly. With bonds as complicated and deep as those between couples, it is easy to hear only what one wants to hear or otherwise misunderstand what is being said. Therefore, clarity is crucial to avoid confusion and more pain in the future. At the same time do not disregard acknowledging the history of the relationship.

※

Liza and Ben began dating in their junior year of college. From the night they met at a mutual friend's apartment through their graduation celebration dinner—which included both of their families—the two were inseparable. After graduation, Ben was to begin medical school and Liza would intern for a publishing firm a few states away. The two decided to give a long-distance relationship a try.

Where once they'd spent days curled up together in Ben's living room or studying and eating at their favorite college joints, now they shared nightly phone calls that left them both exhausted the next day. In addition, Liza's social life suffered from the guilt she felt whenever she went to bars or parties without Ben. She began to feel as though she was living a double life—one spent with her new girlfriends and at the firm, the second on the phone with Ben reliving memories and trying to picture what his medical school and his new friends were like. Liza was growing increasingly envious of her friends who had no emotional restraints. She was also increasingly worried that the time she spent on the phone with Ben was not only affecting her work but limiting her experiences in a new city.

During her upcoming visit home, she decided to end her relationship with Ben. While she would always care deeply about Ben and wanted him in her life, she knew that the long distance was taking a toll not only on her happiness, but also on his ability to be as successful as possible in medical school. She was close friends with one of our office interns and came to her for advice. That advice led to drafting and revising a script that acknowledged their romantic history and brought it to an end—at least for now.

Ben,
    The last two and a half years you have been my best friend. Our times together have been filled with fun and

sharing. You made my college experience very special, but we have taken different paths, and now it's phone calls and frustration. I don't want to see either of us end up hurt, and believe it's best to bring this chapter of our lives to a close before we begin to develop negative feelings toward each other. [Be ready for a reaction that requires: "I understand how you feel."]

So I've concluded since we live apart, it is best we separate ourselves romantically. ["How do you feel?"] This may be the end of our going together, but I hope we can stay in touch from time to time.

Ben was initially upset, but in time he came to understand why Liza had decided to end their relationship. A few weeks later, he saw a significant improvement in his classroom performance and had more time to devote to his studies. Liza was happy as well. Not only did they remain on good terms, but she was able to fully immerse herself in her new city and internship. Ben subsequently started to date a fellow medical student, and Liza is still looking for Mr. Right.

Keep in Mind:

- Start with your appreciation of the history of the relationship. Focus less on personalities and more on circumstances.
- Be prepared for feelings of rejection or abandonment.
- Ask your partner what his or her opinion is. Allow him or her to vent, grieve, or be angry without losing control of your own emotions.
- Hold the line if the separation is your decision.

Making Amends

We can't undo history when we make mistakes. But we can do the next best thing by acknowledging and responding to our errors.

Almost all of us at some point regret saying or doing something hurtful to a friend, loved one, or professional acquaintance. It might be a comment made in the heat of an argument. Or an offhanded, insensitive remark. Or a willful act intended to inflict emotional or physical harm.

Often, the act gnaws at us afterward. That's often a sign that an apology is in order. But it's important to know how to apologize the right way. We've all heard bad, forced apologies. They seem to smack of insincerity.

How many times have you heard these?

- "I'm sorry you feel that way," which isn't an apology at all.
- "I want to apologize for anyone I've offended," which is too vague and doesn't communicate contrition or acknowledge that any error was made.
- "I am sorry, but I was [insert excuse here]," which is a way of rationalizing, but not truly assuaging hurt feelings.

The best apologies are heartfelt and specific. They often involve some soul-searching: dissecting what happened so that the words in the apology can squarely hit their intended target.

Sending flowers can help, but a gift is not an apology in and of itself. It is too nonspecific.

The timing can be complicated. Backing off a hurtful statement immediately can elevate the tone of an angry debate. Sometimes, however, it's best to allow some time and distance to provide perspective before apologizing. "Making an apology is a very serious thing and should not be taken lightly," says author Beverly Engel. "Therefore it is very important that you plan and prepare for your apology in order to maximize the possibilities of it being a positive experience for both you and the person you wronged."

✳

Earlier in my career, a business associate came to a meeting and expressed feelings about wanting a bigger piece of the pie of a company I had founded. It was my perception that he had done little to justify it. Without filtering, I became angry and let him know—in a manner I later regretted—that I believed his request was wholly unwarranted.

I later wished I could have taken back my trigger words, which provoked a threatening response. If I had to do it again, I might have asked him questions to gain a better understanding of why he felt as he did. That would have had the dual benefit of eliciting information about his position and letting him know I was listening.

I couldn't get a do-over of the initial conversation. But I could script an apology in an attempt to rebuild the relationship. These were the points I felt were important to make:

> I was wrong in reacting to you as I did at last week's meeting, and I'm sorry. We might have different perceptions, but I needed to listen more to you so I could understand why you feel as you do. We should have spent more time talking and I accept responsibility for that. If we disagreed, at least we could be confident that we heard each other out.

Since the initial conversation had occurred in person, it seemed appropriate for the apology to also occur face-to-face. We set up a lunch.

While the meal began with strained feelings and small talk, it moved to my expressing the points in the script and ended with a heartfelt apology that I considered an important step in the right direction.

Please accept my apology for any hurt I may have caused.

Although our relationship was not restored fully to its prior level, lines of communication were open again and the tension that filled the room whenever we were together began dissipating.

Keep in Mind:

- Be specific about who you are apologizing to and why you are apologizing.
- Remember first to dissect what unfolded as best you can so you can pinpoint where things went wrong.
- Make sure you accept blame in your apology and do not pass it off to others. If you are not genuinely remorseful, the apology will not be sincere.
- While you might consider a token of friendship (flowers or a gift, for example), it is not an apology by itself.

Rejecting a Friend's or Relative's Request for a Loan

Most of us can remember countless times when we asked our parents for a few bucks for the movies or to pay for a dinner with friends. Sometimes they obliged, but sometimes they told us it was our responsibility. While you may follow this pattern with your children, the situation becomes more complicated when a friend or relative asks you for a loan. The decision must be made whether it is appropriate to provide the money or to deny the friend's or relative's request.

Without the right script, it is possible that the person who made the request will be offended by a denial. Just as bad, you may be too uncomfortable to refuse and may make the improvident loan. If the denial is made too awkwardly, the relationship could suffer permanently.

Scripting a denial will allow you to think through your rationale as well as communicate an effective and diplomatic rejection. Handing out loans to family members and friends may not be a good idea, even for individuals such as famous entertainers or athletes whose net worth is publically available and who have ample means. Often when a wealthy individual gives a loan to someone, even though it's to only a close, credible acquaintance, the lender is bombarded with requests from many others who believe they now also have the right to make such a request.

The underlying objective of scripting a denial is that the decision not be perceived as being made for personal reasons. Rather, the request is denied for beliefs based on an established principle. That principle might be that loans made to relatives or friends can lead to damaged relationships. It might be necessary to assert that once-available funds have been committed elsewhere. In the extreme, if this relative has already been given a loan in the past and has never paid a cent in return, it may be necessary to put a foot down and tell the person to change his or her lifestyle or explore other opportunities.

※

Jack, a seasoned attorney, encountered this scenario a few years ago when his brother-in-law Paul asked him for a loan in order to purchase inventory and equipment for his "can't miss" business venture. Paul was going to revolutionize the health food industry with a line of high-taste, low-fat desserts. As he described his venture to Jack, he even offered to give him a "piece" of his company in addition to repaying the loan "with good interest." Jack did not want to provide the loan because Paul had a history of questionable "can't miss" business ventures that did miss and—on more than a few occasions—had not repaid loans, including one advance made by Jack some years before. Making the loan was a potential "lose-lose" venture for Jack: he would be out the money, and Jack's spouse, Paul's sister, would feel uncomfortably "caught in the middle." Although she sensed the improvidence of her brother's business ventures, she did not want to become involved in Jack's denial of the funds. Therefore, Jack came to me for perspective and advice.

I told Jack to write out a script of what he wanted to tell Paul. When Jack brought me his draft, it needed a lot of work. He used language like "I'd like to help you, but I can't," and "someday I will help, but not this time." In addition to being untrue, the soft language was wide open to be questioned and subject to arguing by Paul. A serial borrower such as Paul would see it as encouragement to continue his efforts to get Jack to give him exactly what he wanted.

As I read over and acted as devil's advocate on the script, I sharpened Jack's language of denial and asked him for some rationales for his response. Since Jack knew Paul much better than I did, he might be better equipped to know what language would ultimately best convince his brother-in-law to accept the denial. After going through the process a few times, we came up with our finished script. Instead of saying that Jack "can't" make the loan, we decided that he should frame his rationale around a generic policy of not making loans to relatives since they have the potential to damage family relationships. Adding a willingness to introduce him to a lender who would provide an objective analysis of the loan request could strengthen Jack's denial while testing Paul's willingness to be measured by conventional loan standards.

Once we'd finished the script, I sat with Jack and assumed the role of Paul as we practiced delivering his refusal. Although he was an estate attorney and not a litigator, Jack's statements sounded more and more like a good trial lawyer's closing argument. Once he was confident with his delivery, he was ready to have his conversation with Paul. Jack was able to communicate his thoughts firmly and diplomatically.

Paul,

I will not make this loan to you and it is important to me for you to understand why not. I have learned that loans to people who are close to you can endanger your relationship with them. While the person may have every intention to pay the loan back when it is made, circumstances frequently arise that make that difficult, and that is when the tensions really rise. [If Paul begins to respond that this deal is different, you may want to say: "Remember the situation x years ago?"] I am not in the business of being a banker, but I will be glad to introduce you to contacts I have at financial institutions in town so that you can receive the benefit of an expert's analysis of whether the loan you seek is appropriate.

[Be prepared for an emotional comeback and be ready to say: "You may not understand this now but I hope you will in the future, and don't forget I am willing to introduce you to contacts at my bank so they can analyze the loan for you and hopefully provide financing to you."]

Jack successfully denied Paul the loan with minimal bad blood despite Paul's initial angry reaction. Jack introduced Paul to several bank officer friends. Although Paul was initially frustrated that he had to rework his pitch to sound more professional, he gained some valuable perspective from going through the banking channels. Although he ultimately did not launch the business, his relationship with Jack suffered no additional strain.

Keep in Mind:

- Bracketed contingent language in a script sometimes helps prepare the communicator for eventualities not initially covered.
- Be flexible. If your spouse or significant other wants to help out a family member, or you simply cannot deny a friend with whom there is a previous bond, try to figure out an approach that minimizes your risk or commitment.
- One possible remedy: offer to match any loan that a bank will give the person, so at least you are not on the hook for the entire sum. In that way, a professional must also judge the investment worthy. This also gives the person more accountability so he or she won't consider the loan a gift between relatives or close friends.
- Be prepared not to be repaid.

Intervening with an Addicted Person

Few families are untouched by the ravages of addiction in one form or another. Substance abuse can undermine the abuser's health and happiness, end friendships, and divide families. Rarely can addicts take steps by themselves to give up drugs. Intervention by loved ones and others close to the addict may be the only means for opening the door to treatment. A common misconception of drug abuse is that the addict must admit he has a problem and desire help. The success rate for addict recovery is the same for those forced into rehabilitation programs as for those who enroll themselves.

Intervening is difficult. Not only is it a conversation neither party wants to engage in, but addicts frequently see nothing wrong with their conduct and come up with excuses like "I don't have a problem" or "I only do it sometimes socially." The intervener must take a position that somehow gets the addict's attention and moves him or her to accept treatment. The very act of conveying to the addict the gravity of the problem may also have a therapeutic effect on the interveners.

The most successful interventions come from detailed planning and uniting all the most important people in the addict's life. Before the intervention takes place, the group needs to meet and prepare the script as well as responses to possible objections the addict may make. Because interveners face an array of emotions and reactions—ranging from stubbornness, denial, or anger to remorse or despair—building some flexibility and counterresponses into the message will strengthen the case for intervention. In addition, expressing affection for the addict rather than anger at how his or her habits have caused anxiety and pain will increase the likelihood of an agreement to treatment.

It is important to spell out the consequences if the addict refuses treatment: for example, an employment contract will be terminated or the addict will need to move out of the house.

❊

During the surge in cocaine use in Major League Baseball in the 1980s, one of my clients, Tommy, demonstrated changed behavior patterns that suggested to me he may be using drugs. When I confronted him about it, he denied having "a drug problem" although he confessed that from time to time he had tried a drug or two socially. Tommy's explanation did not bring me much comfort, but I did not raise any further questions at the time.

Two months later, I was in Chicago and had arranged to have lunch with Tommy before a night game. When I stopped by his room to get him, he told me he needed a few more minutes to finish dressing and I should wait in the living room of his suite. As I strolled around the room, I noticed remnants of some lines of white powder on the glass covering his bureau. When he emerged from the bedroom, I looked him squarely in the eye and asked, "Tommy, what's this?" He hesitated and responded, "You got me, man." Tommy had been snorting lines of cocaine and admitted to his addiction. In order to placate me, he said he would see a doctor and get some treatment.

To the disappointment of me and others, he only went through the motions and did not get the help he needed. His pattern of destructive behavior continued through the following off-season, and I sensed that before long he would either be arrested or inflict some real damage on himself. It became clear that an intervention would need to take place. We had to begin the process of getting him to go into treatment and staying in it until he had a proper program in place to aid him in his ongoing recovery. An addict is never fully healed.

I called several psychiatrist friends to get advice on how and what I should say to Tommy to effectively accomplish my goal. They admonished me that no matter how effective I was in crafting a message and carrying out an intervention process, the odds were that ultimately I would fail and that his substance abuse would not cease. Nevertheless, I sat with my partner, Michael

Maas, and worked on drafts of a script that conveyed the message of intervention.

Tommy,

You know that we have been together for the last four and a half years and through that period I have always tried to be there for you. I was touched when you referred to me as your "dad" and my feelings of affection for you run deep—I hope that I have demonstrated that. [Have I?]

I owe it to you to have this conversation, because I love you. I truly believe that right now your baseball career and even your life are on the line. Your team is aware that you have used cocaine. And the general manager has informed me that he is considering bringing you in and informing you that the team is going to void your contract and put you on the Restricted List. You might well end up being banned from baseball or having your career ended because of possible criminal prosecutions. [So let me ask you, do you understand that all of this could happen?]

I have talked to the doctors at Johns Hopkins Hospital and they are ready to accept you into a substance abuse program and work with you to help get you to a better place and to get your addiction under control. All that we have to do is pick up this phone and let them know that you are coming and they will immediately admit you.

If we don't get you to the program tonight, then there is nothing else I can do for you and I certainly can't argue to the team that they can't pull your contract or suggest to other teams in the future that you can pass your physical. Your career is on the line, Tommy. Let's call the doctors.

The next day, Tommy entered the program. He stayed in it for a month, but when he returned home during the off-season, he and a girlfriend started sharing drugs again. He had fallen off the wagon and was even using crack cocaine.

I received a call from the general manager to inform me that he'd heard Tommy was once again abusing drugs and that he was ready to take action. I asked him if he would join me in an intervention with Tommy. Using a script similar to the one I had implemented in the earlier intervention but expanding it to take into account the general manager's role, we spelled out the consequences of Tommy not getting his addiction under control in even bleaker terms. We both told Tommy that his career would without a doubt come to an end before the next season started.

Tommy again agreed to enter the program at Johns Hopkins, but this time did so with a genuine concern that he would not be able to play baseball again. Six weeks later, he left the program, and five years after that he finished his baseball career. He continues to recover from his battle with substance abuse to this day.

Keep in Mind:

- Remember that addicts are likely not in a right state of mind. Try not to take what they say personally.
- Explain how the addict's actions are not only harmful to himself but those around him.
- Be prepared for a range of emotions, from stubbornness, denial, or anger to remorse or despair, by having a flexible script with counterresponses to any objections.
- Only deliver the bottom line—the consequences—if the addict still refuses to seek help.
- Communicate that this is a demonstration of your love and not a confrontation.

Communicating Condolences to the Bereaved

Have you ever felt at a loss for words when planning to offer condolences to someone who has recently lost a loved one? While expressing sympathy to the bereaved is a part of life, doing it is more often than not a challenge. Whether the mourner is a close friend or a professional acquaintance, the words you choose may well affect his or her feelings.

There is no "boilerplate" language for comforting the bereaved. What is said to those grieving over the death of a child should differ from what is expressed to one who has lost someone significantly older. Recognizing the need to tailor condolences to each circumstance can help assure that the words are soothing and don't cause unintentional discomfort in a delicate moment.

It may seem awkward at first to write down the thoughts you wish to express, either in conversation or in writing. But doing so allows you to weigh their impact and receive input from a third party before you convey them. Unlike scripting for personal advancement or business, this situation calls for a largely one-sided presentation of your thoughts with typically little response from the griever other than acknowledgment.

✳

The case of JoAnn DeCesaris—the widow of my friend Geaton DeCesaris—illustrates the impact your specific words can have.

Geaton died after a three-year battle with cancer. JoAnn had been a constant in her husband's fight against the disease and was left drained and devastated. At his funeral and during visitations, she found some things people said were more upsetting than comforting. Some of the comments made were based on speculation—such as the assumption that her husband had had lung cancer because he smoked. In fact, he had never held a cigarette a day in his life.

This wasn't the first time JoAnn had experienced inept attempts to comfort the mourning. She had lost loved ones before and, along with her daughters, would reminisce after funerals or viewings about the things people would say. The girls would talk about the uncomfortable exchanges and say things like, "What were they thinking?" or "Were they thinking at all?" JoAnn and her daughters always talked about writing a book on what not to say. So after JoAnn experienced the unintentionally hurtful things people said to her during her grieving period for Geaton, she told her girls that she was finally going to write the book. The phrases and instructive reactions below come from that book, *The Things People Say . . . (What Not to Say)*.

"It's good to see you." This was the most common phrase JoAnn heard from acquaintances she had not seen recently. It caused her to focus on their absence during her husband's cancer rather than their attendance at his funeral.

"I know how you feel." Regardless of the person's own relationship with her husband or the person's own life situation, comparing that experience to her own unique feelings did nothing to alleviate JoAnn's pain.

"God has a plan." This was the initial thought she had when her husband was diagnosed, and by the time of her husband's funeral, it had become redundant and infuriating.

"I just didn't want to see him suffer." This sounded to JoAnn more like an excuse for not visiting her husband than a genuine offer of condolence.

"He was my best friend." JoAnn questioned why the people claiming to be her husband's best friends did not come and support him when he needed them most. Unless you acted like a best friend, it's best to steer clear of claiming to have had a relationship that may not have existed.

"Now you can take time for yourself." JoAnn appreciated the substance of this remark and knew that if it had been said long after the funeral, she may have taken it differently. In her book, JoAnn offered a preferable way to express the same thing:

"Please take care of yourself" or

"You've been taking care of others so much, now take care of yourself."

Scripting can help you thoughtfully prepare for a difficult situation in which you may be called upon to express your compassion sensitively and effectively.

JoAnn also offered several examples of genuine comforting condolences, which could also be an initial greeting. They may guide your scripting for similar situations. Below are a few phrases that comforted JoAnn.

JoAnn, I'm sorry for your loss. Geaton helped me stay positive when I faced adversity in my personal life and I will never forget it. I want you to know I am here to offer the same support to you and your family.

This was the most consoling communication to JoAnn and it came from a close friend of her husband's. It concisely expressed his grief while offering his genuine support.

I'm sorry for your loss. He must have been a great father to raise such strong daughters.

JoAnn appreciated these words from one of her daughter's high school teachers, who was more familiar with her children than with her husband. The statement recognized accomplishments in Geaton's life that would continue after his death.

Soon after I graduated from high school, I lost my father. It was different from the loss of a spouse, but heartbreaking because we were very close. Especially comforting to me was a note I received from a teacher of mine that read,

> I am so sorry for your loss. I know how close you and your dad were. He must have been a great dad because his son has such positive values. I hope and pray that as the pain of the immediacy of loss lessens some, the warmth of his memories will bring you and your family some comfort. Please extend my sympathies to your mother, brother, and sister.

When writing a condolence note, it may be comforting to offer "hopes and prayers." This neither denies the pain felt by the bereaved nor diminishes the uniqueness that they attach to their loss. My teacher's note made such an impression on me that it served as a model for my expressing condolences to others in appropriate circumstances.

There is no exact calculus of comfort for the bereaved, but thinking in advance about what to say can bring you closer to providing the comforting words that someone in JoAnn's circumstance needs. Choosing words artfully does not deflate expressions of concern; rather, it supports the objective of comforting others.

Keep in Mind:

- Except in rare circumstances, do not suggest you understand others' grief or what they are going through.
- Take a few moments to jot down some thoughts and reflect on their potential impact.

- Approach the bereaved with a genuine offer of support, as opposed to seeking comfort from them.
- If you are unsure of your words, have someone who knows you and the bereaved look at your thoughts and offer suggestions.
- Sometimes a hug means as much as the words you speak.

Talking to Someone Who Is Terminally Ill

It's been said frequently—and by many people—that there are no do-overs in life. We might occasionally have the opportunity to tread again over old terrain to try to make circumstances right. We might revisit a breakup with a significant other or try a second time to explain a business decision to a colleague. But sometimes we simply don't get second chances. There are few situations with more finality than talking to someone who is very sick and doesn't have long to live. You need to get it right the first time.

It's hard to imagine a better use for scripting than crafting a message to someone who is terminally ill. These are conversations you may end up replaying in your mind for the rest of your life and they can be opportunities to say things you have never expressed to the person—a parent, a significant other, a dear friend. They are also opportunities when the person can communicate important thoughts to you.

It's important to be precise in your language so your message is understood. But it may be even more important to know in advance exactly what topics you want to cover.

A key is not leaving out anything important. There's an old aphorism that regret comes not from what we said, but what we didn't say. You might have always wanted to express gratitude to a parent for standing by you at a particularly hard time.

It's best, of course, not to leave the most important discussions—the issues—until the end. Exhaustion may overtake the person and deny you the opportunity to communicate what you want. You need to gauge what the person can understand in his or her condition, and what he or she can tolerate. Unless you script a plan for what you are going to say, you might fall into the trap of putting off the most challenging communication to the end of the conversation—a common tendency.

And you need to be a good listener—maybe the best listener you have ever been. According to caregivers, people on their deathbeds sometimes need permission to let go. They often go through checklists: Will my children be okay without me? Have I tended to my will? Is there an important issue I have left unresolved? You can listen to them, reassure them, and help them tie up loose ends. And you can make certain you understand how they want to be remembered after they are gone.

My writing partner Jeff Barker has talked to hospice workers and they say that whether the terminally ill are in a hospital, in a hospice, or at home, there are simple ways to calm and comfort the dying:

- Music: Music can set a soothing and uplifting mood and often seems to foster reflection.
- Humor: Telling jokes can be liberating. There is no rule against using humor in a dark situation—quite the contrary—but you should allow the other person to take the lead so you can assess what is appropriate.
- Familiar things: Old family photographs, paintings, flowers from the garden—these items can envelop the terminally ill in good memories.

The idea is to use scripting as a platform for being prepared. But being prepared doesn't mean monopolizing the encounter. After some spontaneous small talk to warm things up, it's a good idea to let your loved one know that you want to hear from him or her before you have your say.

✳

Janice's aunt Susan had lung cancer. The doctors said she might live another month. When she heard about the diagnosis, Janice—who, as a girl, had often spent summers at her aunt's beach house—promptly bought a ticket and a short time later boarded a plane and flew to New England to visit Aunt Susan in hospice.

She was relieved that she had a two-hour plane ride—and another hour in a rental car—to brace herself. She needed time to think over, jot down, and recite to herself all that she wanted to say.

This is a partial list of what she had on her notepad after making several rounds of revisions:

Being with you again makes me think of our wonderful summers together when I was in high school. I remember how we took long walks and I asked you a hundred questions, which you always answered. Do you have any special memories? . . .

I want to say thank you for all the time you spent with me when I was a teenager, and for all the advice you gave me.

I want you to know how much I love and appreciate you. I love you and you are and always will be in my heart.

Is there anything you need me to do for you or you want to share with me? [Cue her to say anything she would like. Consider putting on some music to create the right mood for reflection.]

By the way, your nurse and doctors really sing your praises—what a great patient you are. Can I ask them anything for you? Is there anything else I can assist you with?

Janice shared these thoughts with her aunt that day. When she left the room both she and her aunt smiled at each other.

The doctors' prognosis was correct. Aunt Susan lived three more weeks and then peacefully died.

In the years that followed, Janice felt gratified that she'd made the visit and had warm feelings of that day in Susan's hospice room.

There was one part of the conversation that Janice was particularly grateful for. In the process of saying thank you, Janice shared with her aunt something else she had in her script notes: that she hoped one day to have a daughter and give the child the middle name Susan. Janice's first child was a girl named Jennifer Susan.

Occasionally, Janice felt sad that her new daughter couldn't meet Aunt Susan. But by telling her aunt of her plans for the baby's name, she felt as if she had created an enduring connection between her aunt and her daughter.

Keep in Mind:

- Allow the sick or dying person to drive the conversation. If the person is unable to communicate, just be there for him or her.
- Share a memory or two, and ask for the person's memories or let him or her react to yours.
- Be as specific as possible in your expression of gratitude if appropriate.

- Offer to assist with any issues or needs the person may have—people he or she wants to see, medical issues, estate issues, burial or service plans, etc.
- Create a mood—perhaps with music or flowers or family photographs—that feels comfortable.
- Script in advance the most important topics to discuss and how to present them.

CHAPTER 11

✳

Consumers

Obtaining a Service or Product below Market Price

Limits on spending are nothing new to the many who have not only themselves to support, but also a family. Budgets are established in order to avoid accumulating debt. Purchasing a service or product below an offered price may be an essential piece of keeping the budget intact. It is not necessary to trick or bully service or product providers into reducing the price to achieve this. Rather, it may be a matter of clearly expressing your limitations and being sensitive to the providers' business by offering them something in return for the below-market sale.

Occasionally, products that were once considered luxuries come closer to being viewed as necessities. Responses to recent apparent environmental changes offer an example. Whether the result of global warming or not, few would argue that we are living in a time of increased weather extremes—ranging from ice storms in the winter to blazing heat in the summer, and tornadoes and hurricanes in between. Therefore, when the weather forecast calls for a thunderstorm, hurricane, ice storm, tornado, or other potential hazardous weather, thoughts turn to the power outages that have caused millions of Americans to suffer days without air-conditioning, heat, water, refrigeration, and proper lighting.

After the extreme weather events of 2012, demand rose for generators to lessen the impact of extended losses of power. Installing a generator is not cheap. It can run into the thousands to tens of thousands of dollars. This decision, in a sense, is discretionary. Yet in the minds of many, the need for the product becomes compelling. The challenge then becomes both finding the funds and making the purchase at a price that fits your budget.

❄

In the summer of 2012, the Baltimore-Washington area was hit by a weather event known as a "derecho," an unpredictable and fast-moving storm with hurricane-force winds. Over a million people in Maryland were left without power following this sudden storm. Some lost power for over a week. My family was fortunate; we had installed a generator in our home after an ice storm the previous winter, and we were thankful that— although we were without power for almost a week—limited air-conditioning, lighting, and refrigeration were still part of our lives.

Early one morning in the week following the storm outage, I was in the locker room at the gym, and a conversation among a few friends quickly turned to the subject of generators and their pros and cons. During this discussion, I mentioned how happy I was with our generator and the relief it had brought our family during the power outage. I also answered questions about wattage capacity, cost, and installation.

A few weeks later, one of my gym friends, Andrew, approached me about the challenge he and his wife were facing with respect to purchasing a generator. Andrew was a local school administrator with two young children and an elderly mother-in-law who lived in their home. Although he and his family lived a comfortable life, the funds they could spend on a generator that would adequately address their needs could not exceed $10,000.

Andrew presented his predicament to me. Phil, the generator provider he had chosen, had given him a quote of $11,500. He was unsure what to do since he could not squeeze the $1,500 difference from his budget. Nevertheless, Andrew was desperate not to repeat the misery his family had experienced during the last storm. I told Andrew that he ought to communicate to Phil that $10,000 was all he had available and was thus the limit. I also explained that, in this situation, he must make it clear that he was not in a position to negotiate—that $10,000 was his limit. I told him to e-mail me something that evening outlining what he would say to Phil under the circumstances, and I would have some thoughts for him the next morning.

Reading Andrew's script that night, I knew it needed some work if he wanted to make Phil understand the necessity of meeting his budget needs in order to reach a deal acceptable to both sides. He was inclined to tell Phil he could only "offer" him $10,000 and that he hoped Phil would accept his "proposal." I explained to Andrew that the use of words like "offer" and "proposal" would communicate to Phil that they were engaging in a negotiation. Consequently, the script had to be tightened so Phil would not be likely to think that Andrew had more to offer. I also thought Andrew should consider offering Phil something in return for the reduced price. So Andrew and I came up with a new script, which he practiced before he talked to Phil:

> Phil,
>
> My wife and I appreciate the proposal you have given us and we would really like to work with you, but we cannot exceed our budget for this expenditure. We are only able to spend $10,000. We hope that there is still a deal that would benefit both parties at this number. Perhaps if you are currently tied up with other work, you could schedule us during a less busy time for you and that way fill a period that might not otherwise be productive.
>
> Phil, we would also be glad to be a reference for you to our friends and throughout our neighborhood. We hope it will still be worthwhile for you to do this installation for us. We want this to work for you as well.

I saw Andrew at our gym again about two weeks later, and he informed me that the installation of his generator was to begin the following month at a price of $10,000. Several months later, their generator was put to good use when Andrew's family lost power at their residence for four days. Andrew had not only become a hero to his family, most notably his mother-in-law, but also to several friends to whom he had referred Phil for their generator installations.

Keep in Mind:

- Use language that makes it clear to the service or product provider that you have reached your financial limit.
- Think of something you can give or do in return for the lowered price.
- Remain appreciative and deferential throughout the message.

Receiving Reimbursement or Replacement
for a Defective Product

How many people have bought a new refrigerator only to find its temperature fluctuates unpredictably? Or realized a newly purchased computer's toggle switch doesn't work? Or given a remote-controlled toy to a child only to find it stopped working after a month? In these situations, even if the item is not under warranty, most consumers want to communicate their dissatisfaction and receive a reimbursement or a replacement.

The item may have displayed problems from the start or shortly after its warranty expired. Either way, the malfunction is likely to cause frustration—and a keen desire to have the seller swiftly remedy the problem at no additional cost.

But it can be an uncomfortable situation for buyers to deal with a company's return policies—and perhaps their own discomfort with such confrontations. Engaging in the scripting process may help buyers to feel empowered and communicate a message that is both clear and professional, increasing the chances for a satisfactory result.

Before drafting a message, the seller's return policy should be carefully researched. The policy will offer valuable information on how the seller may respond and exactly what it is required to replace or reimburse. If questions arise or the policy is unclear, the next move may be to call a representative of the seller to seek further information and clarify its stance. The consumer should review the item's warranty (which could mandate a cumbersome return process and require the consumer to deal directly with the manufacturer rather than a retail outlet). Applicable consumer laws and the experiences of others dealing with the seller should be considered as well.

It may be more convenient to deal initially with the seller rather than the manufacturer. But be careful. You need to make certain you don't proceed in a way that abrogates the warranty.

A side benefit of drafting a script is that it can allow the consumer to vent pent-up emotions and frustration. But the final message should be free of emotional language. The customer service representative did not cause the merchandise to be defective. The message should be built on a foundation of civility. Delivering a disrespectful message may backfire by making the recipient less inclined to help. Having a gatekeeper on your side increases the likelihood that this person will apply extra effort on your behalf.

That being said, the consumer must convey an authoritative tone. Word the message succinctly—recite the facts of the purchase and the defect, the harm or inconvenience you've experienced, and supportive information from your research (such as warranty information, if applicable).

While scripts are frequently used to prepare for an oral presentation, this sort of consumer complaint is usually best spelled out in an e-mail or letter. That's especially true if there have been unsatisfactory efforts to get the problem resolved in person. A written message enables the consumer—who presumably has a limited connection to the seller—to state the case unemotionally and with clarity. The message should include copies of all receipts and similar documents, as well as the names of other representatives to whom the claim has been addressed. You might also copy others on the communication—people who are in the seller's chain of command—particularly if the experience or research suggests that the seller is the sort that may need an extra push.

Time is of the essence in such consumer matters. Many

warranties contain time limits. Even when they don't, it's best to report problems swiftly so that the seller feels some sense of urgency and responsibility.

※

A few summers ago, Carla, my good friend and associate, purchased a range for her kitchen for $1,794.12. She excitedly anticipated cooking elaborate holiday and other celebratory meals for years to come. Carla cherished childhood memories of helping her mother prepare Thanksgiving dinners and was eager to start doing it on her own.

Unfortunately, Carla quickly discovered that the range was defective—the oven would not hold a set temperature. After she had multiple protracted conversations with the seller's customer service representatives, the company replaced the faulty range with the same model.

But again, she experienced problems with the range. Owing to the frustration Carla had felt while replacing the prior one, she decided to let it slide and deal with life's more serious issues. But after a month or so, the range's problems worsened and Carla, for a second time, had to face the tedious process of seeking redress.

She called the seller again several times, but the second range was neither repaired nor replaced. Becoming irritated, Carla reached out to me and shared her frustration. I suggested she write out what she would communicate to the seller's representative, assuming someone would listen to her. She gave me an initial draft full of anger and frustration. I suggested toning it down and including the merchant's president and counsel (whose addresses were available online) in addition to consumer relations representatives.

Carla took the emotion out of her script, structured it into a letter format at my suggestion, and made sure to include a detailed account of the time she had already spent expressing her dissatisfaction to the seller. This provided a solid foundation for her request for a full reimbursement of the cost of the original range—plus her desire to have the defective model removed free of charge. While revising her letter, Carla also made sure to take out any language that might seem abrupt or rude.

Below is the message she ultimately scripted and sent in letter form.

Dear [General Manager]:

I am writing this letter to you because I purchased from your store a range for my kitchen which turned out to be defective. Its oven was virtually unusable because it could not hold a set temperature. For over a year, I have sought assistance, but received no redress or satisfaction with your customer service. I will try not to bore you with my personal anguish during this twelve-month nightmare, but please know it has not been pleasant and has reflected poorly on your organization. Here is the timeline . . .

August 2009: I purchased a PB654RPWX range.

December 2009: after numerous frustrating attempts to rectify the issue with your customer service representatives, I finally did receive a replacement of the defective range with another PB654RPWX range.

In January 2010 I discovered similar problems with the replacement range. I wanted to seek redress again promptly, but after the stress I had to go through to get the replacement (defective) range and having to deal with other more serious priorities, denial was my mode of action.

In August 2010 I finally found the courage to face the challenge, again, with the second defective PB654RPWX range. When it was not repaired after numerous service calls (done without charge, but none successful), and the same problems continued with the oven temperature—it could not be maintained—I finally realized that the service I was receiving was not going to resolve my problem.

In twelve months, I have had two ranges and each has been defective with no fix in sight. I therefore ask you: do you feel that this is acceptable? This is more than any customer should experience . . . not to mention all the phone calls (minimum of fifty minutes on hold most times with "please continue to hold . . ." every fifteen seconds), explaining my problems to each new representative, service calls, time off work, and on and on . . . and countless ruined meals including a disastrous Thanksgiving.

At this point, I hope you can sense my frustration with all that I have endured (as stated above, and much more) and will arrange for the range to be returned and to reimburse my $1,794.12, which would cover my original purchase price. I have been a long and loyal customer of yours and hope that that loyalty and my indulgence in this matter will be treated fairly.

Please confirm receipt of this letter by phone or e-mail. I would hope that a speedy resolution can be reached in this matter and that I do not have to take it to the State Consumer Protection Division. Thank you for your attention.

cc: [Seller's President],
[Seller's Counsel]

Certified mail, return
receipt requested

Carla's frustration built over the next month, as the only product of her effort was a green Postal Service card acknowledging receipt of her letter. She then received a response from the general manager (copied to the president) that initially made her gasp. She was informed that the replacement stove was no longer under warranty and that she would not be reimbursed for the purchase price. Her desperation turned to hope when the letter continued by acknowledging her frustration—and her years as a loyal customer—and offering her a store credit that could be used for "another and different stove or any other products" in the store. She was also informed that she could keep the range or return it, and that the store would arrange pickup "at no cost."

It wasn't the precise resolution she desired. But Carla ended up with a countertop convection oven and an upright freezer, in addition to a range with working cooktops—and, I might add, a nice Thanksgiving dinner the following November.

Keep in Mind:

- The scripting process can help develop a sense of empowerment and communicate a message that increases the likelihood of a satisfactory result.
- It's best to start by researching the company's return policy, the product's warranty, and applicable laws on the sale of defective products.
- Speak with respect. It's both what you say and *how* you say it. You're unlikely to get help if the seller's representative feels disrespected.
- Provide documentation, including the specific times you spent interacting with the company to rectify the situation.
- Be clear about the defect and the resolution you expect.

- A letter or e-mail to a manager or executive may be better than phone calls—particularly if no satisfaction is obtained within a reasonable period of time.

Making an Offer on a House below Asking Price

Many highlight reels of adult lives include a scene focused on the realization of the American dream: taking ownership of a home. Buying a house is often the most important purchase in a person's life. The price you ultimately pay is significant for a number of reasons. Every dollar you save on the purchase price can reduce the funds required for the down payment, the money you owe on the principal amount of the loan, and the interest you ultimately pay on the loan. Making an offer below the asking price is not unusual, but it can make some potential buyers skittish. It's important that the buyers overcome any fear of rejection that could cause them to lose their nerve. The scripting process can anchor a buyer's confidence and increase the odds of finalizing a purchase at an acceptable price.

*

One of my associates at our Negotiations Institute, Nate, and his fiancée found the condominium of their dreams near Baltimore's Inner Harbor. From the unit's terrace, they had a view of the water and a lovely park nearby. While most potential bidders, according to the sales agent, tried to take advantage of their time spent with the seller to explain why they were the best candidate for the condo, Nate used his time with the seller differently. What follows is the scenario that unfolded, as Nate tells it.

"When I went to meet with the seller, I did not speak too much about myself. Instead, I sat with the owner and his spouse and, following the probing principles I learned at the institute, just asked questions and listened: Why are you selling the apartment? Where are you moving to and why? What is important to you in this transaction? What else? What else? What is most important and why? By listening carefully, I discovered how important timing was to them. It turned out the couple had bought an expensive house with the intention of making a few modifications, but had gotten carried away and begun a major renovation. As a result, the house was going to take substantially longer to return to livable condition and the couple was unsure as to what they would do in the meantime.

"When it came time to submit offers, I kept in mind what they had told me and scripted out an offer that provided a below-list price but also took into account their timing concerns. I extended the close date by several months and added a thought about being flexible in order to let them comfortably get settled into their new home. I was not in a hurry to move, I just wanted the right place at the right price. Knowing they were in slightly over their heads with the renovation and wanting to ensure the sale would go through, I included a larger-than-average deposit. My total bid, however, was about 5 percent lower than what I was informed by my agent was the highest competing bid.

"I never would have obtained the information I needed to craft my script had I not probed. When my fiancée read over my draft, she suggested I include a note about two apartments I owned that offered short-term leases at reasonable prices—friends of mine had used them in the past and raved about the value. After combining her insight with what I had already written and using my agent as a devil's advocate, I made our proposal several days after my initial meeting with the sellers:

I have thought about our conversation earlier this week and have come up with an idea that might satisfy both of us. I know you have some work to do on your new house, so I am prepared to put off a closing date for four months. I want you to get into your new home as smoothly as possible. If that time period doesn't work, we have several apartments nearby that you could look at as an insurance policy.

We love this home and what you have done to it. And while we cannot pay your asking price, we are prepared to give you a firm contract for $475,000* with no contingencies and the extended date for closing I have discussed. What do you think?

* This was $50,000 below the asking price and $10,000 below what Nate was willing to pay.

"It turned out my bid was 4 percent lower than the highest offer, but it was accepted. I came away with the best property I had seen in over six months of searching. Similar to many other situations, the price was important but it was not everything. By asking the right questions, we figured out what was most essential to the other side and found a way to give it to them without sacrificing our main needs. Two weeks after the sellers moved out, my fiancée and I enjoyed a lovely meal seated at our terrace overlooking the beautiful Baltimore Inner Harbor."

Keep in Mind:

- If time permits, probe before you script the message.
- Information you find out through probing may indicate needs or interests of the seller that you can offer to meet, to make up for offering a lower price.
- Know at what point you will walk away—script a price that leaves room for a counteroffer that is still acceptable to you.
- Practice the scripted message to deliver with confidence.

Negotiating Early Termination of a Lease

Have you ever faced the challenge of terminating a lease before the end of its term? The economy may have changed, you may be moving to a new city, or the location may no longer be satisfactory for your living or business requirements. Whatever the reason, the message you must deliver is not one the landlord is inclined to appreciate. In order to effectively terminate the lease with minimal repercussions, what you say must convince the landlord that giving you your release is the proper thing to do.

Although you may encounter difficult negotiation, find a way to make a lease termination palatable for the landlord. Offer ideas, including your participation in finding a new tenant. Also clearly explain the circumstances and consequences of your need to terminate. The script should make it clear that you are not walking away from your financial obligations.

While the script may not ensure success or even elicit a response, it at least raises the probability of a satisfactory resolution.

❋

My friend Jennifer operated a pet supply business in a middle-income neighborhood. Unfortunately, her business struggled, unable to compete with pet superstore pricing. So, rather than continuing to pump money into a lease for a nonproductive business, she sought a way out. She asked me to read the lease and see if she could terminate. I advised her that not only was there no termination right, but also that she had personally guaranteed the lease. Due to her limited means, she now faced the possibility of both personal and business bankruptcy. It was then that I recommended she go to her landlord and ask if she could end the lease before it ran to full term. I suggested they might come to an agreement that would give the landlord something and allow Jennifer to move on without going through bankruptcy.

I recommended that she leverage the fact that her lease was below market value and that the landlord might well find a lessee at the current market rate. This would provide the landlord with a rational justification for releasing her from the agreement and remove her looming threat of bankruptcy. If she was unable to accomplish this, she would attempt to gain the landlord's approval for her to seek out a sublessee. Her final script, ultimately expressed in a letter, combined a request to end her lease with a proposal that could be mutually beneficial.

Dear [Landlord],

I would like to discuss with you an opportunity to re-lease [the property].

I'm overwhelmed with responsibilities to my family, [the store], and my other job, and after carefully considering my options, I have decided to shut down [the store]. It cannot compete with the pricing of a pet superstore.

I understand that my current space should rent for more than I'm currently paying. And if you agree to release me from the lease, I will do everything in my power to assist you in finding a tenant who will pay the higher market rate.

However, if a market-rate tenant isn't located within thirty days, I would like to try to sublease the space, subject of course to your consent. Because of my dire financial circumstances, my concern is that I won't be able to carry the space through the term of the lease and might have to seek bankruptcy protection. Again,

while I would prefer the scenario that releases me from
the lease, my current obligations to you take precedence,
and my thinking is that I may need a sublessee to help me
fulfill those obligations if we can't lease it to a new tenant
at a market rate. I hope you will help me find a mutually
beneficial solution to this problem.

After Jennifer met with her landlord and delivered this message, he agreed to shorten the terms of their agreement if she
found someone to rent the space. Although he was at first resistant to the idea, he appreciated her honesty and her suggested
solution. If Jennifer's replacement left or failed to pay the rent,
Jennifer would have to pay the balance. It turned out to be a
satisfactory resolution. At the beginning of the next month, Jennifer was confident that the new tenant—whose store would sell
baby clothes—would be able to pay the rent. The sublessee
stayed beyond the term of the lease, and Jennifer never had to
make any additional payments to the landlord.

Keep in Mind:

- Be prepared for the landlord to be apprehensive about the
  news, and comfort him or her with solutions.
- Do not be surprised if the landlord's initial answer is "pay
  the rent." Explain logically why it is difficult for you to
  honor the lease and the consequences of your doing so.
- Do not become emotional if the landlord is not initially
  supportive—remain calm.
- Alert the landlord to the situation as early as possible.

Getting an Upgrade

Sometimes, in travel, you just have a lucky day. The coach section on your domestic flight is overbooked, and you are offered a first-class seat. You strike up a conversation with a hotel desk clerk about the weather and end up being given a suite because of a late cancellation.

To those sorts of scenarios, you say "thank you." But you don't have to rely on dumb luck. Receiving free or paid upgrades—like making money in the stock market—can be influenced by events completely out of your control. But it tends to work out a whole lot better when you arm yourself with strategies. In other words, smart travelers can make their own luck. The most savvy voyagers come equipped with information—and scripts of a sort. Consider the upgrade game like any sport—you have to know the rules about how upgrades work. For example, air travelers will want to know if the wait list is basically first come, first served, or if the airline is giving preference to passengers in the upper-tier, frequent-traveler categories.

Much of your success will hinge on your people skills. It amazes me how often travelers are condescending to gate agents and hotel clerks—the very people with control over upgrades. The courtesy, empathy, or appreciation you show a gatekeeper can go a long way to increase the odds of success. In fact, civility, and empathy with a harassed worker's plight, may in some cases get you the upgrade without ever even having to make the formal request.

The right gatekeeper has a real impact as well. I know a man who shops around for the most amenable customer service representatives when he calls airlines seeking upgrade deals. If he encounters a surly or unhelpful representative he will politely say good-bye and call back hoping for someone more cooperative. As much as possible, you want these interactions to be pleasant.

It also pays to be opportunistic—you might have leverage and not realize it. Consider an airline that has overbooked and can't find enough passengers to switch to a later flight. Yes, the representatives are offering vouchers, but this might also be a time to negotiate an upgrade. Or consider a car rental agency having a slow day—maybe it's Christmas Eve or a day in which bad weather has forced multiple flight cancellations. Those are good days to receive upgrades. Overcome doubt about making the ask by invoking the Old English proverb: Much is lost for the want of asking.

Additionally, there are considerations in seeking upgrades that you may not have thought about. An article from the financial website Bankrate.com explains that the way passengers dress can affect their success at obtaining upgrades:

"If coach is overbooked, but there are empty seats in first class, some passengers may receive an upgrade. It's only natural the crew would turn to someone who looks like they belong there." In other words, you should look—and act—the part of a first-class traveler.

※

My partner in this project, Jeff Barker, once witnessed the following scene at an airport check-in counter:

Passengers were milling about before a cross-country flight when the gate agent announced that she had a few very generously priced first-class upgrade opportunities available. Not surprisingly, more passengers were interested in upgrading than there were first-class seats.

Two men—let's call them Richard and Tom—stood up and headed for the counter to inquire about first class. They arrived in front of the agent at the same time. The agent smiled and said: "Wow. You guys were in a race and it ended up in a tie." As Tom offered his name for a wait list, Richard made a joke—something about how he would rather be drinking champagne in first class than choosing between peanuts or pretzels in coach. The agent laughed. Richard got his name on the list, then returned to his seat. Tom lingered at the gate. He argued that he should get an upgrade because he believed he had technically gotten his name on the list before the other passenger—a debatable point. He belittled the agent and kept other passengers waiting in line behind him by refusing to sit down.

So which passenger got the upgrade? It was Richard, the polite one. My strong suspicion is that the gate agent had enough flexibility to make the call on her own. All else being equal, it's human nature for airline employees to reward people for courtesy.

Upgrade scenarios for air, hotel, and rental car companies are varied enough that there aren't any specific guidelines for passengers to follow. But that doesn't mean you can't be prepared with a script of sorts. The idea is to ask questions that will elicit as much useful information as possible. Here is a list of model questions you might use, depending on the circumstances.

Ask about hotel upgrades:

Does your rewards program include priority for upgrades at a certain point level?

Are you (the desk agent) able to offer upgrades independent of a rewards program?

If an upgrade is not available immediately, can I split my stay and move into a suite when one is open?

Can you put me on a wait list and alert me if there is a cancellation?

I've also learned that any cordial conversation with hotel clerks is better than no conversation in the upgrade game.

Ask about airline upgrades:

Is there a discounted upgrade available since the flight is
about to board?
Can an upgrade be paid for with points or only with
money?
Would there be better opportunities for an upgrade on
the next flight?

Did the airline's delay cause you to miss a business meeting or family dinner?

I'm afraid I missed our firm's meeting today. I'd feel better about it with an upgrade.

Sometimes it may help to sympathize with a stressed-out agent:

I know delays can be unavoidable. Rough crowd you've
got here today, right? Dealing with people in situations like this has to be stressful—I hope I'm not adding to your stress.

So you may not be going through a formal scripting process
to get that upgrade—just be ready with a few good lines, and treat
others as you would want to be treated under the circumstances.
Be cordial and courteous.

Keep in Mind:

• Understand when you have leverage. Airlines, hotels, and
rental car companies are less hassled on slow days and more

likely to have the inclination—and the flexibility—to offer upgrade deals.

- Know the rules of the game—such as when your frequent-traveler status puts you at the head of the line.
- Be prepared to ask questions that may help you understand how you might get the upgrade.
- Be nice—charming even. Nobody likes feeling bullied. And courtesy or empathy may bear dividends.

Protecting against Overzealous Contractors

Paying for an equipment upgrade, landscaping, or other services for your home can have an entirely different feel than most other purchases—such as, say, buying a car. It's somehow easier to be talked into an unplanned expenditure for a home improvement project that feels important even if it is over your budget. It's an easily rationalized purchase, as it's something that you will appreciate every day and "enjoy for a lifetime."

The problem is that you may then find yourself in a financial hole. An HVAC upgrade; landscaping improvement; windows, doors, or siding replacement; generator installation; and other projects may start with addressing a specific need. But in the end, these can all open the door to unnecessary and costly add-ons. A salesperson can make you feel you simply must have this "one more thing" despite the adverse budget impact.

Consider what usually happens during a home services transaction. Typically, you and the provider walk through your property to analyze how to address a need. The representative may point to one thing or another that "could really be improved" and add to the home's appearance and value.

The salesperson's excitement—without any discussion of costs—makes the suggestion appear irresistible. So you climb aboard the expanded home improvement bandwagon. Unfortunately, the significance of the added cost only strikes you later when you receive a bill or write the check for the product or services.

Many of us have a proclivity for such impulse buying. Investing time in a script can help you focus on your limits and prepare you for a sales pitch.

The script can generally be simple and brief. The message should reiterate the specific job you want done, as well as your budgetary limits. It's best to be as explicit as possible in explaining that you cannot spend more than you planned. If you like the company, you might propose extending the relationship into the future. The most important thing is to have a few words in mind before the meeting so you can avoid having the discussion move to an expanded inventory of work and costs.

❄

Our neighbor, Patty, worked hard to make her serene "farmette" property attractive and livable. She was proud of its appearance and pleased with the peace and quiet it offered her and her family. After a recent storm, she felt that certain trees on the property—particularly those adjacent to the house—needed pruning and in a few cases removal so as not to pose a hazard in the event of future storms. The third arborist she invited to the property had a reputation for doing excellent work. He addressed the matter with a clear and effective plan that was close to the budget that Patty and her husband, Sam, had set.

As he walked away from the house, however, he pointed out to Patty that a number of other trees "could also use some work" and "would really look great" after pruning. He explained that the work would help preserve the life and well-being of the trees. He told Patty that since they would be working on the trees around the house, he would be happy to take on the additional work "at my cost"—in other words, a reduced rate for Patty—as it would give his men some work to do during the off-season. Patty, excited at the idea of enhancing the property further with additional work done at cost, gave him the go-ahead.

When the work was done, the trees and property looked great. The problem was that what had been anticipated by Patty as $5,000 worth of work had resulted in a bill of $9,000. Her reverie about the beautiful result faded with the realization of how much she had spent. When she and Sam had dinner with us later that week and described what had happened, she asked how she could have avoided it and how she could prevent her impulsive ways from being exploited in the future.

I told her about my idea for this book on scripting, which I was contemplating at the time, and how the scripting process could help people choose the right words to—among other things—protect them against yielding to unwise consumer temptations like the expenditure she had just experienced.

I explained that she could ponder the visit of a home services or product provider in advance and prepare a script to keep her purchases under control. As we talked through dinner, we scratched out on the back of an envelope what that script might have looked like for dealing with the arborist:

> I really appreciate your coming today. I am very interested in solving the problem of the trees around the house and having them cleaned up and pruned so as not to be a threat to the house or unsightly after future storms. Can you tell me what you estimate the cost of that work will be? [Wait for response and then reiterate:]

Let me emphasize that our budget is $x and we are just about at that number on this project.

[If other work is pitched:]

I appreciate your ideas. They are good ones. Maybe we can consider some of them next year when our budget is not so tight. Thank you. When can you start the work on the trees around the house?

Patty looked at the script on the envelope and said, "Wow, that would have done it, and it might have helped with a few other projects I've undertaken in the past."

When I gave Patty a copy of this chapter to read, she said she is still waiting for an opportunity to put scripting into practice. I asked her to let me know the result.

Keep in Mind:

- The message should be concise and reiterate the specific job you want done as well as your budgetary limits.
- Consider suggesting the possibility of pursuing the new suggestions another year.
- Preparing your thoughts before the meeting can help deflect having the discussion move to an expanded inventory of work and costs.
- Be cordial, but firm.

Gaining Admission to an Exclusive Group

At one time or another, many of us aspire to join an exclusive group. It might involve being admitted to a school, club, housing cooperative, or fraternity. Applicants—particularly inexperienced ones—often struggle with a balancing act: how to present themselves in the best possible light without overselling, exaggerating, or coming off as arrogant.

Some begin at a disadvantage—they simply aren't comfortable talking about themselves. They might have very specific ideas of how they could fit into the school or club they hope to join. But their apprehension prevents them from articulating their vision to the people they need to influence.

This is where scripting can help. Not only will the scripting process help provide a game plan, but it can also embolden the applicant in an interview setting in which they don't want to sell themselves short. A script should be a source of information that resonates with decision makers. It's not enough to say, "You will be glad you accepted me" or "I will try hard" or "I will make this work." Specificity is key. The college admissions process provides a clear example of this. Admissions officers often say the most memorable applications offer vivid portrayals of the students— describing their experiences, say, going on safari, volunteering at a homeless shelter, or directing a short film—in high contrast with those that offer only support statements like "I have had experiences that make me ready to take on college." The best applicants not only describe themselves, but also use examples to illustrate their points.

※

My former student Robert agreed to buy an apartment in a tony co-op. The purchase was contingent upon approval of the co-op board.

This board's members were firmly entrenched and had clearly delineated ideas about who they wanted in the building. In their minds, all of the entrants had to be quite wealthy and over fifty years old—much like the board members themselves. Robert, an investment banker, filled out an application but was uncertain if he would qualify because of his age, thirty-two. The board members wanted applicants with demonstrated "maturity," which they felt could only be achieved by someone of their more senior years.

When Robert came to me for help, I told him to try to put himself in the board members' position. "Think about why the requirements are important to them," I said. "And think about how you see yourself qualifying. Tell them a story about yourself."

That was what Robert did. He gave me a script that I minimally touched up and then he made his case to the board.

I can understand that some of you may be uncomfortable with a thirty-two-year-old moving into this wonderful building. If I were you, I would wonder about his financial ability to maintain his unit and pay co-op fees. I might also wonder about his partying habits.

Well, let me put your minds at ease. When I was ten years old I started a business breeding cows on our property—a gentleman's farm—in suburban Philadelphia. The business made money and I was able to help my parents with the cost of my education. People called me "mature beyond my years" and that continues to this day.

In addition, my current job allows me to make well more than your minimum income requirements (you have my income tax returns) and my long working hours make the possibility of partying in my unit impossible. [Can I answer any questions for you?]

I want you to know that in me you have a candidate—though a bit younger than you—who you will be proud to call a neighbor.

Robert closed his interview by describing his fondness for the building. That was clearly a sentiment that would be shared by the board, and the board did approve his application. Ironically, he never moved in. It turned out that exterior cracking led to leaks into his unit and damaged the walls and floors. Robert then exercised his right to opt out.

But his preparation had allowed him to feel guided and in control of a process that can feel intimidating.

Keep in Mind:

- Put yourself in the position of the decision makers and imagine what they need to hear.
- Don't sell yourself short, but don't oversell to the point of creating skepticism.
- Use concrete examples from your background to illustrate why you would be a good fit.

Epilogue
A Case Study in Avoiding Excuses

As valuable as scripting can be—not only in negotiating business deals but also in difficult conversations with family and friends—I invariably encounter people who push back and try to circumvent it as part of their preparation. Among the scripting skeptics are some CEOs and other high-level organizational leaders I have worked with. In many cases, when it came time to sharpen the message they were to deliver, they would tell me they "knew how to do it." They had plenty of experience, they said, in making their case and did not need to go through the three-Ds process to come up with the right words to achieve their objective.

Yet on more than a few occasions, the result would be a point carelessly made—or at least not expressed with the same level of precision or confidence that had taken place in our preparation discussions.

Most would learn their lesson quickly and take to scripting in their next round of the discussion, and in significant interactions thereafter.

I've heard other excuses for bypassing scripting. One (discussed in my book *Dare to Prepare*) is popular with people from all walks of life—they just "don't have the time." Often, however, their presentation will miss the mark and they'll spend even more time engaged in trying to rectify their mistake.

Just as I resisted learning how to use the computer a decade ago because I "didn't have the time" and "knew how to do my job" without technological support, these people resist incorporating the three Ds in their business and life tool kits. Hopefully this book—and some experience in applying it—teaches the lesson I learned when I finally relented and dove into the digital world. Not only will they perform their job more effectively, they may also wonder how they managed before embracing the scripting process.

As I was writing this book, I assisted in a business transaction that illustrates why I believe scripting can be such an effective tool. It shows the benefits of scripting, but goes a step further by describing the perils of not scripting when the pressure is on and the stakes are high. I think we can learn as much from an example in which someone resists scripting (at least initially) as from one in which a person meticulously scripts. As in earlier sections of the book, the names and facts have been changed out of concern for privacy.

❋

A company, Perfect Products, was considering relocating from New Jersey to Michigan, which had offered significant inducements. While the company found the Michigan idea tempting because of reduced labor costs and improved distribution capabilities, the firm had a long history in and strong connections to New Jersey. Michigan was offering a traditional package of low-interest loans, a choice site, and relocation services.

That package by itself would not be enough to convince the company's board to approve the move. The board members recognized that the company's officers, key employees, and family members had strong ties to the New Jersey communities in which the company currently operated. Cultural institutions and other boards were populated with the company's people. In addition, the company's founders and some present-day leaders had deep roots and strong political involvement in New Jersey.

Nevertheless, Perfect's CEO, Theo Best, a brilliant leader who had joined the company two years earlier (after leaving his role as COO of another consumer products company in Illinois), saw great advantages for the company in making the move. He and his CFO projected profitability and growth possibilities from the move. At the same time, they had decided that in order for Best to sell the move to the company's key board members and other stakeholders, the company would have to receive more than the traditional package offered by the relocation state. It would also need an outright relocation grant in the amount of $50 million.

That $50 million payment would help defray some of the significant costs of the move. It would also help reduce the capital burden that the company would face in the conversion of the Michigan site to serve Perfect's needs. Perhaps most important was Theo's recognition that he needed to secure such a payment to get his key constituents on board.

To complicate matters, Theo feared that if he requested an outright grant rather than the low-interest loan packages suggested by Michigan officials, Michigan might move on to another prospect.

I was called upon by a board member to help Theo and his team negotiate with the Michigan Economic Development Corporation team assigned to bring Perfect to Michigan. After receiving and reviewing a briefing book and financial analysis Theo's group had put together, I met with them to strategize and discuss the impending negotiation.

My partner, Michael Maas, and I were asked to coach the Perfect team through the negotiation process. They felt comfortable that Michigan would provide a "most-favored nations package of inducements," but were uncertain about the prospects of achieving the outright $50 million payment. That was an inducement Michigan had never offered before.

They understood the tremendous impact the deal would have on Michigan—offering the opportunity to revitalize an area of the state that had precipitously declined with the contraction of the auto industry and its ancillary businesses. Theo and his team knew Michigan had other opportunities, but felt none would affect the state as much as Perfect. A meeting with the state negotiation team was set for the next day and there was concern that if Perfect and the state did not come to an agreement quickly, Michigan would move on. The Michigan team had implied that strong possibility in a phone call earlier in the week.

It did not take long for me to recognize the brilliance of the CEO and his ability to absorb information. He quickly grasped data and strategies presented to him and confidently came to rapid-fire conclusions. I did sense, however, that it might be difficult to get him to engage in full-scale scripting for his discussions with the state's officials. When I suggested scripting out what he intended to say, he told me—and his team reaffirmed—that he was quite used to collecting information from experts and communicating it without scripting. He used speeches he gave as an example. Clearly he knew how to deliver an important message effectively. He described himself as a "mental scripter," saying, "I do not have to write anything out."

He asked what I would recommend that he say in the next day's meeting and reminded me that he had limited time to prepare. He said he would absorb the message and was even willing to orally present it back to me, Michael, and the assembled group.

But there was no convincing him to write out a script and have us act as his devil's advocate before the meeting. He also would not practice his presentation in more than a cursory fashion; I retreated to describing what he should say. When I finished my presentation, one of his team remarked that she was convinced the message was pitch-perfect.

What I said went something like this:

> We want to find a way to make this happen. If we do, then Michigan and Perfect will both come out winners. Our company will be able to achieve new levels of business and profitability by relocating and Michigan will gain a real strong stimulus for its economy and tax base.
>
> But this will not be easy for us with the strong history in New Jersey and the tremendous ties we have developed there. We need more than the relocation package you all have put together. In addition to that package we will need an outright grant of $75 million to support the breakup fee New Jersey will ask of us as a result of our not fulfilling certain loan covenants we signed on to with them as well as to help us defray some of the capital needs we will have for some special plant features to build out for our manufacturing and supply chain processes. We hope you understand the uniqueness that Perfect brings to Michigan. It will give you a large high-growth employer unlike any you have ever brought to the state before.

After I made the pitch, Theo's house counsel seemed impressed. "I'm convinced," the counsel said. Theo, however, voiced reservations about the $75 million ask. "That will certainly scare them off—I may not be comfortable doing it." I then explained the "aim high with reason" principle. I said that he could certainly justify the number and could expect them to negotiate down any number we offered. Theo said, "You're the negotiation expert—I got it."

I asked Theo again if he would like to write out the statement and have me play devil's advocate to better prepare him. He said he was comfortable without writing it out and asked if we would be available for check-ins and consultation during the meeting the following afternoon. Michael and I agreed to be on call. I closed the meeting with a reminder of the Old English proverb I mentioned in the last chapter: Much is lost for the want of asking.

It was time for the big negotiating meeting and the question was, how exactly would Theo execute making the ask? Only Theo, David (Michigan's team leader), and David's counsel met for discussion; they did this in a room adjacent to the conference room where the rest of the Perfect team members were assembled. The team could hear the conversation, but not participate in it. Perfect's counsel made notes of what she heard.

When Theo came back to the room, his group sensed something was not right. Theo reported that it had all gone almost too easily. David had told him that, while he wanted to review with the governor and his team, he would be inclined to support the idea of providing Theo with what he had requested.

But Perfect's counsel then spoke up. It seemed there had been some miscommunication. "I am afraid he did not hear you the way you wanted him to," the counsel said. Theo asked what she meant. She responded that—while Theo did reference $75 million—what he'd actually said was: "We will need financial support *in the range of* $75 million—somewhere between $50 and $75 million to sell this to our board." David had then responded: "So if we can expand our package with additional financing in that range, we could have a deal?" Theo responded in the affirmative.

Perfect's counsel continued to replay the all-important conversation in her mind. To her, David seemed to have been talking about expanding the package of loans but not making an outright grant. The specific grant request had been conspicuously missing from Theo's presentation. Theo shrugged his shoulders and said, "Let's call Ron and Michael."

During our conference call, Theo expressed concern that the counsel may well be right—that because he had not specifically asked for the *grant*, David may have thought he meant debt financing.

"I suppose I was not precise enough," Theo conceded. He was even less comfortable when I told him that his retreat to the $50–$75 million range may also have set the bar below $50 million. I explained that people always hear the piece of the range most favorable to them and negotiate from there. Theo responded: "What do we do now? He is supposed to get back to me later this evening." I asked if he was willing to do a little scripting. Being a man who does learn from his mistakes, Theo responded that he would.

We then proceeded to put together a script to overcome any miscommunication over what terms Theo needed from Michigan if he was to make the move a reality:

> David. Let me be clear. We have spent a lot of time getting our board to buy into this. But that buy-in is unconditionally predicated on our receiving the package you previously

outlined plus an outright grant of $75 million. Michigan's investment will be more than repaid quickly with the jobs, tax revenues, and community commitment that Perfect brings to it—unequaled by any other prospect you might consider.

As he practiced his delivery with us, Theo again expressed reservations about the $75 million and repeated that it might be a "real turnoff for them." I reiterated the underlying negotiations principle that the script was founded upon, and Theo agreed to respond to David as planned. And Theo then volunteered: "Staying in New Jersey for now is not the worst of alternatives."

Later that evening, we received a call from Theo in which he described David's initial elation at being able to get the "loan package" expanded for Perfect by $40 million. Theo then told us that he had delivered his now-scripted message, and that David had suggested that they would have to move on to another prospect. Theo had then delivered a line we had prepared:

> Well, if that's what you have to do, we understand. We have a good situation with New Jersey and will stick with it. But if you change your mind, let us know.

After Theo spoke, David thanked him and suggested they stay in touch. Theo asked me what I thought, and I responded that he had done well and that my experience told me that David would be back. And David did come back with several counterproposals, including one that Theo—and the Perfect board—approved. It included the $50 million grant from Michigan. After their final deal-clinching meeting, Theo e-mailed me:

"Mission accomplished. $50 million in grant money now part of the deal. Thank you."

It took some doing, but after getting a rare second chance, Theo eventually saw the utility of scripting. Like many of us, he had initially resisted because of his confidence in his communication skills and inherent time pressures. But he learned how drafting, devil's advocacy, and delivery practice can perfect a pitch in situations where there may be little margin for error. Hopefully reading this book and using the three Ds and its other lessons will cause others to lay their excuses aside and use it as a guide to find the words to achieve success in many of life's important challenges.

Acknowledgments

It took heavy doses of encouragement, support, and advice to complete this book. It had been five years since my last book, and I faced a daunting schedule. Was I ready to take on another project and the responsibility and deadlines that go along with it?

My encourager-in-chief, my wife, Cathi, reminded me of how much satisfaction I get from empowering people by having them engage in the scripting process so they can achieve the best result in their interactions with others. Her words along the way made her a supporter as well as encourager.

Joining her in the lead role in the cast of supporters was Jeff Barker, who assisted me not only with his writing, but also with questions that made me ponder how I was delivering my message. And my partner and friend Michael Maas, with whom I shared the experiences that provided many of the scripting stories, jumped in with ideas and editorial comments from the earliest stages of this project to its completion. My thanks also go to Greg Jordan for his significant contribution to the introduction of this book, as well as to my agent, David Black, for understanding the project and leading me to another key supporter, my editor, Caroline Sutton.

Other supporters included interns at the Shapiro Negotiations Institute, who took on any and all requests I tossed their way to make my job a bit easier. Isabelle Schein was a star among them as she dedicated herself to getting things recorded and written for me as the starting point for writing many of the model script chapters. In addition, Ryan Gisriel and Jack Parchman did whatever they were asked—from research to writing and organizing material.

The best supporting intern, or perhaps better described as "Most Valuable Player," was Hunter McIntyre. When I wondered whether we had the capability to assemble and organize material, verify statements, or just plain meet deadlines, I turned to Hunter. He unflinchingly took on the task, spent untold hours, and cleared my route to the goal line.

And finally this book is better because of friends who were willing to hear ideas or read all or part of the manuscript—while offering advice along the way. They include: Joan Abelson, Frank Adams, Joel Beren, Kim Brock, Joann Davis, Larry Gibson, Rick Haggen, Kim Jackson, Todd Lenhart, Dennis Mannion, Bekah Martindale, Bill McComas, (who also supplied valuable legal advice), George Mister, Steve Mosko, Carl Roberts, Paul Sandler, Joel Sher, George Stamas, Ed Brown, and Lou Trotter. And thanks to the alumni of the Meyerhoff Scholars at UMBC, who took time out from a program I was facilitating to brainstorm ideas for a title for this book.

As a postscript, but not an afterthought, let me recognize a special category of contributors—the two people who have assisted me in all of my professional roles. The first is my executive assistant at our law firm, Gloria Dausch, who—after supporting, encouraging, and advising me for more than twenty years—retired as I was writing this book. And then there is my right arm and jack of all trades at the institute and also the law firm, executive assistant Kim Talbott. Without them and all they take on, this book might never have seen the light of day.

RMS, Butler, Maryland, 2013

Notes

CHAPTER 4

41 **On the day the deal was announced:** http://bleacherreport
.com/articles/335615-no-new-deal-for-mauer-but-twins-are-
optimistic.

ABOUT THE SCRIPTS

55 **While the model scripts should not be used verbatim:** To
protect the privacy of my subjects, I have, in most cases, changed
their names in the background stories, and in several cases have
altered the facts of the story.

CHAPTER 7

110 **The offensive action has the power to affect its targets' psychological mind-set:** "Sexual Harassment: Myths and Reali-
ties," *Journal of the American Psychological Association* (2010): n.
pag. Print.

114 **Your file should contain a written response:** http://www.ny
times.com/2005/06/26/business/yourmoney/26advi.html?_r=0.

114 **"You need a written record of your dissent":** Ibid.

119 **"Life is too precious to spend another minute of it with
you.":** Cited in Stuart E. Weisberg, *Barney Frank: The Story of*

America's Only Left-handed, Gay, Jewish Congressman. N.p., University of Massachusetts Press, 2009.

CHAPTER 9

138 **The fiancé or fiancée should be informed:** Jacqueline Newman, "Approaching Your Fiancé (or Fiancée) about a Prenuptial Agreement," Berkman Bottger Newman & Rodd LLP, www .berkbot.com, 26 June 2012. Web.

138 **This result would inhibit discussion:** Kirby Rosplock, "7 Tips to Overcoming Prenup Paralysis," GenSpring Family Offices LLC, Winter 2010. Web.

138 **It can be helpful to begin the discussion:** Ibid.

138 **If one has accumulated, created, or inherited wealth:** Ibid.

139 **At the end of the initial delivery, the fiancé or fiancée should be given time:** Ibid.

142 **Often, a vague response can satisfy a young child's prying questions:** "Sex Education: Talking to Your Teen about Sex," Mayo Clinic, Mayo Foundation for Medical Education and Research, 18 Nov. 2011. Web.

143 **Discussing sex should be viewed as an ongoing conversation:** "Sex Education—Tips for Parents," Home, Better Health Channel, July 2011. Web.

143 **Parents and teenagers may find the topic easier:** Ibid.

143 **In order to create a comfortable setting, parents should avoid disputing:** Ibid.

148 **"As a parent, you're left with the question":** http://parenting .blogs.nytimes.com/2012/12/15/how-not-to-talk-with-children -about-the-sandy-hook-shooting/.

152 **"In the final analysis it is not what you do for your children":** Lin, "Boomerang Kids: How to Kick Grown Adult Children Out of the House," Telling It Like It Is, www.tellinitlikeitis.net, 29 Mar. 2010. Web.

156 **32.9 percent of failed marriages are caused by financial problems:** M. G. Cleek and A. T. Pearson, "Perceived Causes of Divorce: An Analysis of Interrelationships," *Journal of Marriage and the Family* (Feb. 1985): 179, 181.

159 **Research has revealed that divorce:** Shendl Tuchman, "Five Considerations When Telling Your Children You Are Getting Divorced," Good Therapy, 3 Mar. 2011. Web.

159 **Communicating to children a separation or divorce decision:** Larry Carlat, "How Not to Tell Your Kids You're Getting Divorced," TheHuffingtonPost.com, 8 Mar. 2011. Web.

160 **If possible, wait for both parties' outward emotions to cool:** "Divorce: What to Tell Your Children," Family Education, n.d. Web.

160 **Because of the strong bond that children generally share with both parents:** Ibid.

160 **Initially, parents can prepare for this:** Ziba Kashef, "How to Tell Your Child You're Getting a Divorce." The Baby Center. N.p., n.d. Web.

160 **Planning a message that neither places blame nor dwells on many details may help:** Tuchman, "Five Considerations When Telling Your Children."

160 **Parents might try to establish what their children already know:** Jocelyn Block, Gina Kemp, Melinda Smith, and Jeanne Segal, "Children and Divorce," Helpguide.org, Nov. 2011. Web.

161 **Deliver the message clearly:** Kashef, "How to Tell Your Child."

161 **Keep the conversation simple to avoid confusion:** Block et al., "Children and Divorce."

161 **Offering clarity as to when the official separation will take place:** "Divorce: What to Tell Your Children."

161 **In addition, it's critical to emphasize to children:** "Children and Divorce," American Academy of Child and Adolescent Psychiatry, n.d., Mar. 2011. Web.

161 **Inform them that the divorce is not the result of their actions:** Kashef, "How to Tell Your Child."

168 **Weller's vehicle went almost three hundred yards:** "89-Year-Old Found Guilty of Manslaughter," CBSNews.com, 11 Feb. 2009. Web.

168 **Drivers over eighty are more likely than others:** "Taking the Keys Away from an Elderly Driver," National Safety Commission Alerts, 18 Feb. 2009. Web.

168 **While surrendering the keys might be a matter of basic logic and safety:** David Solie, *How to Say It to Seniors: Closing the*

Communication Gap with Our Elders. New York: Prentice Hall, 2004. Print.

169 **Telling a respected adult that he or she has become inept:** Connie Matthiessen, "Stop Driving: How to Talk to Elderly Adults about Giving Up the Keys," Caring.com, 17 Jan. 2013. Web.

169 **You will want to convey that you understand what this sacrifice means:** Harriet Vines, *Age Smart: How to Age Well, Stay Fit, and Be Happy.* N.p.: Aeon, 2008. Print.

169 **Options such as creating a carpool schedule:** Matthiessen, "Stop Driving."

169 **you can raise the possibility of completing an unsafe-driver report:** Depending on one's residing state, ParentCare Pro provides a useful resource to determine how best to complete a report with the DMV (https://www.parentcarepro.com/state-by-state-eldercare-legal-forms-and-templates-2/download-form-to-notify-dmv-of-unsafe-drivers). The Insurance Institute for Highway Safety has a helpful guide that clearly explains each state's laws concerning elderly drivers (http://www.iihs.org/laws/olderdrivers.aspx).

169 **That may be the inevitable close to the conversation:** "Taking the Keys Away from an Elderly Driver."

CHAPTER 10

180 **"Making an apology is a very serious thing":** Beverly Engel, "How to Give a Meaningful Apology," University of Massachusetts Amherst's Family Business Center. N.d. Web.

187 **The success rate for addict recovery:** "Tough Love or Love First?" *Counselor* (31 Jan. 2003): n. pag. Web.

187 **The most successful interventions come from detailed planning:** Ibid.

187 **expressing affection for the addict rather than anger:** Ibid.

190 **He continues to recover from his battle:** Some of the facts in this story have been altered slightly to further protect the identity of the subject.

CHAPTER 11

205 **If questions arise or the policy is unclear:** http://www.bbb
.org/blog/2012/12/bbb-tips-to-ease-the-holiday-gift-return
-process/.

205 **The consumer should review the item's warranty:** Ibid.

205 **Applicable consumer laws and the experiences of others:**
http://lifehacker.com/5853626/how-to-return-nearly-anything
-without-a-receipt.

206 **the consumer must convey an authoritative tone:** Ibid.

218 **"If coach is overbooked, but there are empty seats in first
class":** http://www.foxbusiness.com/personal-finance/2011/08/
18/five-cheap-ways-to-fly-first-class/.

INDEX